CW00673512

'Charlie Bell's *Queer Redemption* is a beautiful reminder that queerness is not just a gift for LGBTQIA people, but that queerness ultimately helps theology – including Anglican theology – to be true to its own stated aim of faith seeking reason. This is important reading for all who love the Church and who hope for its redemption.'

The Revd Dr Patrick S. Cheng
Visiting Professor of Anglican Studies
Union Theological Seminary in the City of New York

'Every so often, a person of faith comes along to prod and provoke the rest of us to stop taking small opportunities in our faith communities to be mean and, instead, to be brave in taking large opportunities to be generous. Only with such disturbing grace can our communities become places of genuine belonging rather than venues where people are made to merely "fit in". Charlie Bell is such a person. If he continues to help us all self-scrutinise as Christians, and grow in spiritual intelligence and human empathy, as he does in this book, then long may his provocation thrive!'

The Very Revd Dr Mark Oakley
Dean of Southwark

QUEER
REDEMPTION

QUEER REDEMPTION

How queerness changes everything we thought we knew about Christianity

CHARLIE BELL

DARTON·LONGMAN+TODD

First published in 2024 by
Darton, Longman and Todd Ltd
1 Spencer Court
140 – 142 Wandsworth High Street
London SW18 4JJ

© 2024 Charlie Bell

The right of Charlie Bell to be identified as the Author of this work has been asserted in accordance with the Copyright, Designs and Patents Act 1988.

ISBN: 978-1-915412-62-1

A catalogue record for this book is available from the British Library.

Printed and bound in Great Britain by Bell & Bain, Glasgow

To Piotr

CONTENTS

PART I
QUEERING THE PITCH

1

MAKING NO APOLOGY

Many of us are sick and tired of talking about marriage. That might sound like a strange line with which to start yet another book on the rights and wrongs of same-sex or same-gender relationships in the church. Pages and pages of ink have been spilt on this most thorny of issues, and still the magic solution has refused to reveal itself. Debate after debate, argument after argument, well-argued thesis after well-argued thesis have been presented, and we remain – in many places – in deadlock. For those of us for whom this is rather more than an abstract 'issue', the whole experience has been bruising at the very least. Many of us have walked away from a church that simply doesn't want us there. Some of us have stuck around to fight. Tragically – a tragedy that cries to heaven for vengeance – some LGBTQIA people have found life not worth living because of it.

The Church of England has made some headway in recent years, although if we are honest that headway is pretty limited – more scraps under the table than radical inclusion. Other churches, too, have begun to realise that platitudinous refusal to recognise queer holiness in their midst is neither sustainable nor, actually, holy, and have made stumbling steps forward in conceding that there might just be something good in the lives and loves of LGBTQIA people. Some churches, of course, are well ahead of the game, like The Episcopal Church in the United States of America, and we can thank God for their witness. Yet even in such churches, there is a tendency to try to fit LGBTQIA people – queer people – into a cis-heterosexual mould, a tendency to deify the cis-heteronormative ideal and find ways of squeezing us into it, come what may.

So whilst this book is, indeed, about marriage – at least in part – it is not solely about marriage, and nor is it yet another argument for concessions for LGBTQIA people. Those arguments will continue to rumble on, but they are inadequate and ultimately unfruitful. Queer people are not called to become honorary heterosexuals – we are called to bring our own gifts to the church, and the church is called in turn to listen to us. We have spent far too long being apologetic – indeed, we have spent far too long doing apologetics. We have spent far too long playing with exhausted material and not nearly enough time listening to the reality of queer lives within the church. It's time for us to unashamedly, unapologetically make the call: the church needs us, it needs to listen up, and it needs to queer up.

The use of apologetics – the use of reasoned arguments to justify something – has a good, long and important history in the struggle for LGBTQIA equality in the church, and I'm not for one minute arguing that apologetics have no role in conversations around LGBTQIA inclusion and affirmation in our churches. However, the ever-present risk is that we end up focusing on precisely that point – inclusion – and in doing so we end up playing the game on someone else's playing field. Whilst the word 'inclusive' has proven useful to some degree, there is a simple fact that we must not ignore: LGBTQIA people are not here to be included in anything – we are already included by Jesus Christ. Those of us who have stuck around in the church, despite the endless attempts to cut us off or cut us out, know this to be true. We are already part of the church in precisely the same way as anyone else is, and a failure to recognise that is not on us. We don't need anyone else's permission to be included.

Now this is not said in naivety. The institutional church is perfectly able to exclude us and to ensure we're not made to feel welcome. It's for that reason that moves towards marriage for all rather than solely for the select few matter – the ongoing refusal of the sacraments to LGBTQIA people is nothing short of a scandal. Yet sometimes we do need to be reminded that for all the institutional church (or indeed for all each different institutional church) thinks of itself as utterly coterminous with The Church, that is plainly false. This very fact should be hammered on the hearts of Anglicans, and yet so often we behave as though the real institutional church just moved on from Rome to Canterbury in 1534. It's simply not true, and our bishops would do well to remember that. Whether they – or anyone else – like it or not, queer people are already in the church. We might just not be fully recognised in yours.

This book is not arguing, then, for a place at the table for LGBTQIA people – that place is already set. What it is arguing for is why recognising that place being set is so important for the vitality of the church of God, institutional or otherwise. It's starting point is not the possibility of same-sex or same-gender relationships, or the possibility of marriage, or any other of the insulting ways of describing queer Christians. It's starting point is that we exist, and that our lives are holy, and – to coin a phrase – the church needs to get over it. We're here, we're queer, and we're not going anywhere.

THE CELEBRATION OF QUEERNESS

It is worth fleshing out that starting point a little more. This book takes as read what we know to be true – from experience, from social science, from medical science, from real lives and from real evidence – about queer loves, lives, relationships, hope and fears. These are no longer up for debate. For far too long, we have acquiesced in our endless debates, allowing those who want us to remain in the shadows, or ideally out the back door, to hold the upper hand. In the name of good disagreement, we have been willing to describe thinly veiled prejudice as theology; we have shied away from calling things out as homophobic, as transphobic, as queer phobic. Just because something is described as theology doesn't mean it can't be homophobic. Yet just as perniciously, we have been willing to allow our bad faith 'debating partners' to suspend reality and call an apple a citrus fruit in the name of theology. We have given far too much credence and air-time to 'theological arguments' built on sand, and in doing so, we have allowed the rug to be pulled away from under us. The time for this kind of pseudo-debate is over.

A brief example might help to illustrate this point. In recent years, there has been a decisive move amongst those who won't see the face of Christ in queer people away from proof-texting, away even from the reproductive essentialism in sexual relationships (of which more later) towards a focus on what Jesus said about same-sex relationships. Of course, Jesus didn't say anything about same-sex relationships, so the argument falls at the first hurdle, but if we buy the initial premise for the sake of argument, then we end up with a protracted debate about Matthew 19, and Jesus' teaching on marriage as he makes reference to Genesis.

Except, of course, it's not really Jesus' teaching on marriage at all – it's Jesus' teaching on divorce, and, to quote the scripture directly (Matthew 19:3), 'some Pharisees came to him, and to test him they asked'. It is fascinating how often the actual context of the verses used to deny the holiness of our love is ignored, in the name of ensuring cis-heterosexualist ideology is untouched. Rather than this being a passage where Jesus straightforwardly condemns same-sex marriage (as ludicrous as that sounds, it is often presented in precisely those terms), this is instead a passage where Jesus responds to a trick question about opposite sex divorce! Those who use this passage to oppose same-sex relationships might, indeed, want to reflect on their own willingness to accept divorce.

Yet this passage is one that is routinely wheeled out to tell those of us who it does not address directly that in it,

Jesus forbids us from falling in love. In doing so, not only is the context ignored, but the nature of the literal (or otherwise) understanding of the Garden of Eden story is also swiftly brushed over – a story which is taken to be myth except, it seems, when a literal understanding enables those who oppose LGBTQIA affirmation to elbow it into their theological arguments. That's not to say that this isn't a passage that has something to say about relationships, or the nature of what happens when two become 'one flesh' (and to use such a task to reject queer relationships and complementarian theology at the same time is quite the feat of intellectual gymnastics). It's also not to say that the Genesis story isn't important, or Jesus' engagement with it, and that it might form part of a nuanced, more conservative reading of scripture. Yet it is to say that the blithe, corner-cutting rhetoric that simplistically uses these passages to demean LGBTQIA people is something that we, as queer people, have all-too-often taken for granted. Biblical interpretation, and its relationships with our already pre-conceived ideas, is complicated, and because of this, the working needs to be shown, whatever position is adopted. We fail to push for it at our peril.

Of course, those of us who push back are told that we don't understand the scriptures, or the more insidious and endlessly trotted out line 'all reputable scholars agree that X', which, of course, relies on one's own judgement for what a 'reputable scholar' looks like – the circular argument *par excellence*. For too long we have thought that if we continue to present reasonable arguments, then eventually people will be willing to concede, at the very least, that we might have a well-argued and intellectually coherent point of view. It is time that we woke up. In their arguments, people will continue to call an apple a citrus fruit if it helps them.

No amount of apologetics is going to help us here. An apple is not a citrus fruit – it simply isn't. If your ideology tells you that it is, then no amount of evidence or argument is going to convince you that it isn't. In many ways, this is the situation in which we find ourselves in church debates about same-sex relationships – and it is fair to say that those of us who believe LGBTQIA people should be fully included in the church also come at this with our own preconceptions, preconceptions we have built in theological ways just as much as those of our opponents. We might think our arguments are better, that our understanding and application of scripture is more rigorous, that our engagement with the theological tradition is more fruitful, that our assumptions are more carefully examined, but our opponents might – and do – say that we're calling a melon a cucumber. We are at an impasse.

Yet there is a simple reason as to why this impasse is not quite as it seems. Whilst these debates will go on and on until the cows come home, one of the most interesting things that becomes ever more obvious as we encounter the usual arguments is not so much the blasé, crude use of scripture to bash people over the head with, but instead the unambiguous refusal of so many who hold to a 'conservative' position to engage with the reality that stares them in the face. Ideologically, there cannot be any good in sexual queer lives, so therefore there isn't good in them – and that is that. This leads to the somewhat absurd position that despite there being very clear, evidenced goods that come from same-sex relationships – fruits of the Spirit, perhaps – these must be rejected because of a prior ideological commitment. All this is dressed up in theological clothing, of course, but it is nonetheless another attempt to call an apple a citrus fruit, and in this case the onus is on those who deny queer holiness to justify their position. To date, there has been an utter failure to do so.

Now this might be something of an extreme position to take and might be reasonably contested as caricature. Whilst some 'conservatives' might indeed oppose same-sex sexually active (a terrible phrase) relationships, nonetheless they might indeed recognise that good things can come out of them. The problem with such a (somewhat illogical) position, of course, is that whilst good things might be coming out of same-sex relationships, nonetheless those relationships are bad in and of themselves – they are sinful, those people are in a state of sin, and for many 'conservatives', that living in sin may well be a salvation matter, endangering people's immortal souls. So whilst there is nuance in the argument, nonetheless we need to recognise that the good that might be seen as fruit of these sinful relationships does no good to the individuals themselves if they continue in their sin – and of course to leave that sin is to leave that relationship, and forego the 'goods' that were incidental to it. In other words, however much good is coming out of a same-sex relationship, the only godly way forward is to end it. That casts rather a different light on the 'goods' that are seen as flowing out of it.

Our premise here is that to ignore what's in front of us is not a good idea. Queer people are good, godly, holy, created in the image and likeness of God just the same as anyone else, and their relationships are also good, godly, holy, just the same as anyone else. This is not a book arguing why that is the case – it is a book building on that simple fact, asking what an embracing of that fact might do to the church. It is not a book trying to argue about melons or cucumbers, apples or oranges. Instead it is saying, given that an apple is so abundantly clearly not a citrus fruit, given that same-sex relationships are so obviously good and holy, what might the church need to do differently to take advantage of this reality. What might we all need to do to really live this reality, rather than simply name it? This book is a celebration of queerness – and a call to the church to learn from the insights that queer lives bring.

QUEER DEMANDS

In our next chapter, we will turn to what queering means and the kind of questions that it will force us to ask – and attempt to answer. At this stage, however, it is worth us simply reflecting that if we are open to such an enterprise, then our entire conception of the church is going to be shaken. This is a good thing. To date, the acceptance or inclusion of LGBTQIA people in churches has quite simply not triggered the kind of questions that need to be asked. Opening marriage up to people of the same sex or gender has not led to an expansion in the church's understanding of marriage to any great degree, despite the fact that such insights are only just beneath the surface. It has not led to any serious challenge to the lazy assumptions and half-truths that the church continues to propagate in the name of 'unity'. In an attempt to keep as many people as possible on board, the wider ecclesial discernment that should have been part and parcel of the recognition that queer loves and lives might just be good has not – in the main – taken place. We need to change that.

The current way of 'embracing' LGBTQIA people, even in explicitly affirming churches, implicitly suggests that there are no insights that queer people might offer to the wider church *as* queer people – the 'queer' is a problem, not a gift. This kind of pedestrian path has not been helpful to the church, and nor has it done justice to the real lives of queer people either. Marriage as an institution is not without its faults, and yet too often our fight for access to this one sacrament has led us to present ourselves as 'close to straight' as we can, in order to show how we might fit into the cis-heteronormative ideal. In other words, we have effectively retained 'heterosexual marriage', and slotted 'homosexuals' into it. This is of little benefit to those of us who are queer, but it is also doing a huge disservice to the church's own process of 'seeking understanding' in theological matters. If we really want to include – or affirm – LGBTQIA people, then we need to listen to them. Of course, many in the church don't want to do either.

We must not forget, too, quite how political so many of these questions have become. In *Queer Holiness*, we considered some of the ways that LGBTQIA people have become collateral, or human footballs, or simply erased from the church. In the Church of England's discernment following the *Living in Love and Faith* process[1] queer people have once again become a matter for debate, with the approval, or otherwise, of their relationships being used as a proxy for 'orthodoxy' within the church corporate. This has led to a process of 'coming up with a deal' over matters of sexuality which – whilst understandable – ultimately leaves many of the deeper, more important questions untouched. Practical questions about discipline and order have superseded the more important questions of anthropology and ecclesiology, leading ultimately to an outcome based more on finding ways to live together without bloodshed than to an enriched and holier church. Many are understandably tired of the primacy given to conversations about sexuality and gender, and yet we might argue that the real conversations have not yet even begun.

A book on queer people and queer ideas will, of course, major on queer matters, and it is absolutely the case that a willingness to think in a queer way is a huge gift to a church that has become sedimented into an outdated form of Constantinian Christianity. However, it is worth raising at this stage that the questions raised by queering the church, and indeed by LGBTQIA relationships, are often questions that apply just as deeply to those who sit within the cis-heteronormative ideal. Queer people have for far too long been the scapegoats for straight people – our relationships have been sensationalised, our sex lives seen as convenient outlets for moral-purity based outrage. Detractors of the arguments presented will, with depressing inevitability, employ slippery slope arguments and use these to colour queer

---

[1] *Living in Love and Faith* has been a protracted period of discernment in the Church of England on matters of sexuality and gender. It describes itself in the following terms: 'How do questions about identity, sexuality, relationships and marriage fit within the bigger picture of the good news of Jesus Christ? What does it mean to live in love and faith together as a Church?' https://www.churchofengland.org/resources/living-love-and-faith [accessed 25th August 2023]

people as inherently depraved and unable to sustain godly relationships. Nothing is further from the truth – unfortunately, truth is often the first casualty of debate.

It is interesting that those in the hierarchy of the Church of England are starting to speak publicly about this very fact, which does appear to be little more than thinly veiled homophobia. The *Church Times* reported the Bishop of Dover as telling General Synod in July 2023 'with barely concealed fury':

> I suspect that if my blood pressure was taken at the moment, it would be off the Richter scale ... Why are we reacting in such a visceral way? What is it? What does it say about us?[2]

The *Church Times* article reports the Bishop of Dover as challenging General Synod:

> all of our children and grandchildren were having sex, she said – but nobody was refusing to walk with them in the Church, or consign them to "an outhouse" ... her heart was breaking as she listened to the conversation under way, she said, at the "callous refusal" to walk together with LGBTQ+ believers ... many of those coming forward for heterosexual weddings in church were living together and having sex, so what was it about homosexual sex, she demanded, that so upset the Church?'

This being the case, it is hard to deny the place of LGBTQIA people as scapegoats in church conversations about sex. Whilst it would be easier to shy away from the difficult questions that follow from an open and honest engagement with matters of sexual intimacy, not least in order to avoid the accusation of a slippery slope, this is not the way

---

[2] Tim Wyatt, *Synod members express frustration at slow progress on blessings for same-sex couples*, Church Times [https://www.churchtimes.co.uk/articles/2023/14-july/news/uk/synod-members-express-frustration-at-slow-progress-on-blessings-for-same-sex-couples]

that theology should be done. As we shall see later in this book, heterosexuals have themselves decoupled sex from reproduction, but have then conveniently ignored this when using reproduction as a key tenet of marriage. There will be no shying away from these matters in these pages, and nor should there be in any discussion of human sexuality. Queer people are not inherently more sexually 'deviant' than anyone else – we just appear more willing to talk in an honest and open way about sex, something that the church could do well to learn from.

QUEER QUESTIONS

The recognition that difficult questions might need to be asked shouldn't be seen as a threat but as a blessing to the church. If we take the holiness of queer people and their relationships as read, then we can finally move beyond a depressing 'what goes where, when and how' way of addressing sexual ethics towards a far healthier, more interesting, and ultimately more theological enterprise. One of the key gifts of queer people is to free the church up from focusing on the peripheries towards a focus on the fundamentals. The old and tired adage that 'marriage is between a man and a woman' ultimately runs the risk of starving the church of its ability to think carefully about the quality of relationship found at the heart of marriage, focusing instead on the mechanics of penile vaginal penetration which seems a poor substitute for questions of relationality.

Once we recognise that the 'man and a woman' element is descriptive rather than prescriptive – that it does indeed describe what marriage has historically looked like but is not necessarily integral to what marriage is ontologically – then we can start asking the much deeper questions about relationship, fidelity, fruitfulness, and so on, that ultimately enrich our understanding of marriage as sacramental. If we hold that marriage is a sacrament, or at least sacramental, then we must surely take that as our starting point – in other words, we must ask what it is that is sacramental within marriage. There may be legitimate questions about procreation and reproduction, but these ontological questions must be the starting point rather than tangential to questions of human anatomy. Queer people help us do precisely this.

Indeed, one of the key gifts of queerness is that the church is set free from its imprisonment to a cis-heteronormative paradigm. We'll cover that more in the next chapter, but for now we might simply reflect on how much of what we call 'Christian' today is actually primarily cultural, whether relating to our own cultural context, that of 100 years ago, or that of 2000 years ago. There is much talk about being 'countercultural' in Christian circles, and yet that concept is far too casually used and far too infrequently interrogated (and as we shall see in Chapter 3, it suggests a monolithic and monocultural Christianity with more than a hint of racist ideology). The idea of the nuclear family being the Christian ideal is anything but Biblical, and yet this particular trope finds a home throughout vast swathes of Christianity.

Marriage, even, is surely not front and centre in Christian living – its value is in its sacramentality, yet it has never been seen as essential for salvation and nor, until recently, as a marker of any form of orthodoxy. As Robert Song puts it, marriage is not 'the epistemological starting point from which we may begin to understand something of the nature of God. And it is certainly not that human efforts at stable relationship are the reality, and the human relationship with God or the inner divine relationships a projection on to the sky that legitimates and stabilises particular human social orders'.[3] Marriage is not the point – God is. Yet in today's church, it seems to be the institution most fiercely protected from queer people.

3 Robert Song, *Covenant and Calling: Towards a Theology of Same-Sex Relationships* (London: SCM Press, 2014) p.10

An almost absurd outcome of this kind of protectionism can be seen in the outcomes of the *Living in Love and Faith* project. At the end of the long period of discernment, the bishops of the Church of England proposed that the doctrine of marriage[4] remain unchanged (although, of course, that doctrine isn't currently embodied in practice given the reality of marriage after divorce), whilst blessings would be made available to people entering into relationships with someone of the same sex or gender. Much argument has been had about these blessings and whether they are truly blessing the couple or the individuals, but it is notable that the main thrust of debate has been about whether these blessings contravene the doctrine of marriage and the importance of the doctrine remaining unchanged. In practical terms, couples can now approach Church of England parishes to receive a blessing on their relationship, whilst the Church of England – for political reasons – will not act as registrars for same-sex marriages. In other words, the part of the service which is specific to the church – blessing – is offered, whilst the part of the service which is shared with the state – the registration of a legal marriage – is denied.[5]

There is not the space here to fully tease out the full bizarreness of this outcome, but it is remarkable that the

---

[4] In the form of Canon B30 (1): the Church of England affirms, according to our Lord's teaching, that marriage is in its nature a union permanent and lifelong, for better for worse, till death them do part, of one man with one woman, to the exclusion of all others on either side, for the procreation and nurture of children, for the hallowing and right direction of the natural instincts and affections, and for the mutual society, help and comfort which the one ought to have of the other, both in prosperity and adversity. [https://www.churchofengland.org/about/leadership-and-governance/legal-services/canons-church-england/section-b] Accessed 25th August 2023

[5] The Church of England, as the Established Church of the Realm in England, has particular civic responsibilities and privileges, which includes the clergy acting as Registrars for marriages. Couples of the opposite sex or gender are entitled to get married in their parish church (with very few exceptions – for example divorce and remarriage) – it is interesting that the majority of the arguments around the doctrine of marriage ultimately relate to this civic role rather than those things which are specific to church weddings (e.g. blessing).

focus of 'conservatives' has been to keep the 'doctrine of marriage' intact rather than make (and hence debate) the quite clear link between blessing and holy living. Bizarre attempts to answer the question 'when is a marriage not a marriage' have been made, including a highly indefensible and internally inconsistent separation of marriage from holy matrimony,[6] and this is the inevitable outcome when a focus on the peripheries and the politics trumps a conversation about the essentials of human relating.

Which brings us back to the starting point of this chapter – many of us are sick and tired of talking about marriage. Marriage is ultimately a sterile tool to have the kind of conversations that we need to have, and until we recognise that fact – and 'we' here includes queer people – then we will continue to have the same drawn-out apologetic arguments. Marriage matters – but it is not the be all and end all, but rather at its best can reflect far deeper, underlying truths about God and humankind. Our starting point needs to be elsewhere.

To end this chapter on a personal note – when I was speaking about the importance of same-sex marriage at an event last year, I was challenged by a brilliant priest in the London area, who asked me what has become a key challenge and a key encouragement for me: 'so is this all just about gay, white middle-class men getting married?'. It took me aback when I first heard it, but she was absolutely right to ask it, and the answer must – if we are to do any justice whatsoever to this topic – be an unqualified, unequivocal 'no'. It is to showing why that 'no' is so important that we now turn. What is this queer thing all about?

---

6 For example, that found here: *Living in Love and Faith: A response from the Bishops of the Church of England about identity, sexuality, relationships and marriage* [https://www.churchofengland.org/resources/living-love-and-faith/bishops-response-living-love-and-faith] Accessed 25th August 2023

2

QUEER?

It's fair to say that the word 'queer' is not met with universal delight.

There are a number of reasons for this, ranging from the entirely understandable to the entirely predictable. For some, the word conjures up the abuse, prejudice and hatred of childhood and teenage bullying, which often spilled into adult life – a term of violence which can never be redeemed. For others, and that often includes White gay men, the term is a step too far, a call to take part in a fight which for them is in many ways over – at least so far as perceptions go. Much easier to be gay than queer, gay having at least somewhat entered the 'normal' in society; sadly it is much easier to see one's own fight for liberation as separable from wider conversations about sex, gender, and sexuality (and the additional intersectional concerns which we will address in the next chapter).

For still others – those who, perhaps, quite intentionally feed the anxieties of gay men – the word queer has become a convenient catch-all that can be used to besmirch anything that doesn't fit into the cis-heterosexualist,[1] patriarchal paradigm as somehow filthy, dirty, other, depraved. It does

---

[1] We will find the words cis-heterosexualist and cis-heteronormative found throughout this book. The former is a system that feeds bias and discrimination against non-cis-heterosexuals; cis-heteronormativity is an assumption that the 'correct' and 'normal' way of human relating is cis-heterosexual.

not take long to find the usual tropes being trotted out, originally applied to gay people, and now entirely unfairly associated with queerness – which quite often end in the accusation of paedophilia and other despicable and clearly unacceptable crimes, which have absolutely nothing whatsoever with being queer.[2] Whilst many have tried to reclaim the word, bad faith actors will never cease in their attempts to ensure whichever sexual or gender minority of the day faces the full opprobrium of uninformed hate (we might consider the contemporary references to 'gender ideology' as an example of this particular genre)[3].

We are using the word *queer* here not only because of the sense of its having been redeemed in much common parlance, but also because of its use in a branch of theology which – if allowed to flourish and grow – offers huge opportunities to the wider church. Its use, however, comes with a few health warnings, which it is only fair to offer up front. For those who are well aware of the wider queer literature, please forgive what may appear to be an unnecessary level of defensiveness over the term: for a church that seems to find using even the word 'gay' a step too far on occasion, and whose leaders (certainly within England) appear entirely unable or unwilling to condemn homophobic or transphobic hate crimes in the same way as other hate crimes, there is – on occasion – the need to use kid gloves.

The first point to make is that embracing the word *queer* will need us to show a certain level of courage. The slurry of confected outrage from the usual suspects can already be heard the moment the word leaves the mouths of theologians, and even in churches who have learnt that LGBTQIA people aren't the monstrous, church-hating heretics we are so often

---

[2]   I am choosing not to supply references here in order not to dignify this kind of hateful bile. A simple internet search will give reams of examples.

[3]   Of course, those opposing 'gender ideology' in this way are often themselves anything but uninformed, and are instead pushing a cynical and well informed strategy, which often includes usurpation of feminist language, amongst other things.

painted to be, it is a rare bishop or church leader who would be willing to put their head above the parapet and talk of queer theology. Yet we should be clear that our use of the word *queer* in this context is not the same as using the words *gay, lesbian, trans* and so on – it comes with wider associations and meanings than simple the description of the sexuality or gender identity of individuals who are not cis-het. Queerness requires a paradigm shift.

We will think about what that paradigm shift means in a moment, but for now the enormity of what is being recommended – and the potential impact of that – is worth paying attention to. Whilst it would be easier to try to elbow LGBTQIA people into already formed categories, behaviours and motifs, queer theology suggests that in doing so we neither benefit them nor the wider church. Thus, whilst there is an unbreakable bond between the lives of LGBTQIA people and queer theology, nonetheless queer theology goes well beyond a simple reflection on identity[4] and asks questions that penetrate the deepness of the theological tradition in its entirety. In a sense, the very existence of LGBTQIA people spurs us onto a recognition that queer theology is needed. As Christians, we can either have the courage to see where that leads us, or we can label it as too scary, too uncomfortable, and leave it there. It's the former of those paths that this book recommends, and it is now time to ask exactly what that paradigm shift might be all about.

---

[4] We should be aware that identities are not formed (and do not exist from thenceforth) in a vacuum and are rather a complex and ongoing interplay between the individual and the corporate. As such, the role of social norms cannot be entirely ignored (even if they are rejected), and nor can identities be seen solely as the creation of the individual. This will mean that LGBTQI identities are anything but fixed even within a particular culture (given cultural heterogeneity) and hence requires us to listen to varying manifestations of queerness. Of course, the ecclesial community, tradition, and expression, also play a role – in the case of LGBTQI people, this has historically been antagonistic, and hence it is not surprising that queer identities are still described as being in opposition to the church (a statement which will contain differing levels of perception and reality).

THEOLOGY OR THEOLOGIES?

Up till now, we have spoken as if queer theology is one thing. At this point, it's worth being clear that nothing could be further from the truth. Queer theologians are renowned for delving way beyond single theological paths, and because of this, the field can feel rather confusing and lacking in clear order. The bad news – for those of us who find order rather appealing – is that that's the point! Queer theologies infrequently attempt to be systematic (in fact, they are usually seen in opposition to systematic theology), and they remain healthily sceptical of anything that might look to be too neatly ordered. This is, of course, their gift – their endless determination to ask questions of God and humankind that do not start from simplistic human-defined categories or delineations. Yet it is doubtless the case that what is offered in these pages is little more than one particular version of queer theology – one exploration based on the seeds of LGBTQIA experience. To that end, it remains contingent, and potentially quite wrong. That is something we simply have to live with.

We also have to recognise that it is the nature of queer theology that it will remain a theology of the outsider. Not all those who write or engage in queer theology are themselves LGBTQIA, and that in itself is not a problem. It is the contention of this book that queer theology has a great deal to offer the wider church, and so we must surely hope that queer theology does not become a theology of the silo. Yet we must also be clear that queer theology cannot become a comfortable theology – nor, indeed, a theology of the comfortable. This is not theology that approaches or attempts to create a neatly packaged God, nor a theology that deals in neatly packaged people. It is a theology in direct opposition and in direct contradiction to an understanding of the world that relies on social convention and forms of enculturated Christianity, a Christianity that sits comfortably in the corridors of secular power and privilege. It is a theology that is constantly challenging our preconceptions, secular or sacred, and that engages us in a constant process of refinement, argument, and disruption. It is a theology that is steeped in the reality of life, that refuses to be domesticated or held to ransom by social convention. It is a theology, ultimately, of life as it is, and not life as the powerful wish it were.

Given that, this is not ever going to be a theology where everyone is going to agree – including its proponents. It is likely to be a theology that scandalises – that says the quiet bits out loud and, in the process, refuses to observe social niceties and refuses to turn a blind eye, however uncomfortable or conventionally unwelcome that might be. It is also a theology that takes human experience seriously, that looks towards what is really happening in the world rather than what would prove most convenient for those in authority, and which refuses to let go of difficult questions rather than sweeping them under the carpet, or making vague reference to theological themes like the Fall in order to silence opposition. It is, at heart, a refusal to say that the way humans see things is the way God sees them – and an attempt to tease out why this might be the case.

Marcella Althaus-Reid, a key proponent of queer theology, was clear that the role of queer theology is to 'interrupt and transform the whole reality within which people's economic and sexual lives and relationships are organised and classified in theological terms',[5] and makes clear the importance of queer theology remembering and owning its place as a disruptive force: 'Terrible is the fate of theologies from the margin when they want to be accepted by the center.'[6] In any institution, and most particularly a religious one whose structure and practice is built on hierarchy, this is an ever present risk. As we

---

[5]   Linn Tonstad, *Queer Theology: Beyond Apologetics* (Eugene, OR: Cascade, 2018) p.85

[6]   Linn Tonstad, *Queer Theology: Beyond Apologetics* (Eugene, OR: Cascade, 2018) p.85 quoting Marcella Althaus-Reid, "Thinking Theology and Queer Theory", *Feminist Theology* 15 (2007) pp.302-14, p.304

shall see, it is an endless temptation of theologians, Christians in general, and perhaps in particular those in positions of religious authority, to baptise social structures or cultural conventions and call them godly.

There remains a sense that the work of queer theology remains suspicious, somehow contaminating, something peripheral and unorthodox, something to be avoided. Yet it is precisely this contamination that wider Christian thought and practice needs – contamination by a source that refuses to move its sight from God to human invention, indeed away from God to idol. Picking apart the places those idols have put down root in what we call theology is surely the work of any serious Christian. Linn Tonstad, in her *Beyond Apologetics* makes reference to Althaus-Reid's work to make just this point, and it is worth quoting her at length:

> Queer … is the very essence of a denied reality …
> [W]e speak of 'Queering' … as a process of coming back
> to the authentic, everyday life experiences described as
> odd by the ideology – and mythology – makers alike.
> Indecenting brings back the sense of reality.[7]

It is this 'coming back to' reality that this book calls us to do. For too long we have spent time arguing – apologising – on others' terms, and because those terms have become so pervasive and so familiar, we have begun to see ourselves as the problem, the issue, the 'unorthodox', to coin a phrase. Yet nothing could be further from the truth. Theology can never be done about things that are not – it can only ever be done about things that are. The things that are include queer Christians, queer lives, queer loves, queer holiness. The things that aren't include the special sinfulness we are told we inhabit simply because we seek love and dare to speak

---

[7] Linn Tonstad, *Queer Theology: Beyond Apologetics* (Eugene, OR: Cascade, 2018) p.98 quoting Marcella Althaus-Reid, *Indecent Theology: Theological perversions in sex, gender and politics* (Oxford: Routledge, 2000) p.71

its name. Queer is an attention to the real, but millennia of Christian enculturation necessitate us doing this through a serious process of interrogation and particular attention. It is to this that we now turn.

WHAT IS QUEER THEOLOGY?

Having laid out some of where the problem lies, it is now time to turn to the fundamental definition – or definitions – of queer theology. As we have said, this is not a singular notion, and nor is it solely about LGBTQI identity, although it cannot be separated from it. Chris Greenough, in his *Queer Theology: The Basics*, grapples with this tension. He makes reference to David Halperin's work, which states that 'queer is by definition whatever is at odds with the normal, the legitimate, the dominant. There is nothing in particular to which it necessarily refers. It is an identity without an essence',[8] yet notes Halperin's development of the idea that queer is 'positionality rather than an identity'.[9] Laying aside the potential issues with the first part of Halperin's argument (we shall engage with the concept of 'normal' later in this chapter and question its utility in such arguments), we can nonetheless feel the strain here between identity and positionality.

Arguments are frequently made (including in Greenough's own work) that 'queer is indefinable',[10] which is presumably because queer theology is ultimately a theology of protest, of challenge, of opposition – as Greenough argues, it is 'fluid; it is unfixable'.[11] There is much to be recommended

---

[8] Chris Greenough, *Queer Theologies: The Basics* (Oxford: Routledge, 2020) p.24 quoting David Halperin, *Saint Foucault: Towards a Gay Hagiography* (New York: OUP, 1995) p. 62
[9] Chris Greenough, *Queer Theologies: The Basics* (Oxford: Routledge, 2020) p.24
[10] Ibid
[11] Ibid

in this approach; however, we will gently challenge this notion, arguing instead that queer, being an active form of attention to reality, does indeed have its own particular essence, indeed an essence that is more 'real' than that which it challenges. It is the normative that is unreal – powerful, perhaps, yet ultimately lacking in reality because it builds dogma on pretence. However powerful and self-referential its proponents, unreal theology remains unreal. Of course, in a sense there is a need for a dialectic approach between these two ways of engaging with the world (and with God), yet they are not equivalent – the normative approach is built on idols which by their nature are immovable, impossible to change, fixed, whereas the queer approach is by its nature one in which a reliance on – indeed, the building of – such idols is fundamentally incompatible with its existence.

Whilst much has been made of 'gender ideology' in the ever-present and ever-disappointing arguments made by proponents of normativity in church culture wars, it is clear that normativity as a theological motif is more truly an ideology than queer approaches, which by their essence remain questioning and challenging. The challenge for queer theologians is to move beyond a playing field that is set by proponents of normativity – in other words, a need to move beyond apologetics. The risk of arguing that 'queer is indefinable' is that it becomes definable only in opposition to the normative – hence ceding the ground on which the dance of theology is played out. This cannot be allowed to happen.

At this stage, it perhaps worth asking an obvious question: what, then, of the creeds? In a sense, this question could be widened to many aspects of Christian doctrine – if queer is an approach that challenges and is 'at odds with the normal, the legitimate, the dominant', then in what sense can queer theology be in any historical sense Christian. There are two possible answers to what is a question of fundamental importance – important not least because of the strength of opposition to queer theology from self-defined 'orthodox' Christians.

The first answer would be to simply accept that queer theology is inherently unstable, and as such may indeed find itself outside the bounds of what might be reasonably considered as Christian. Some queer theologians are perfectly comfortable to hold to this position and there are benefits to it, not least a refusal to play by the rules set down by others, however ancient or venerable those rules might be. We might call this approach the Protesting Queer approach – one in which even those things held to be essential to the nature of Christianity are up for debate.

An alternative approach is to situate the process of queering intentionally within the Christian tradition, yet doing so without taking for granted the current manifestations of Christian truths, and in a way that intentionally challenges the assumptions and peripheral expression of these truths. In other words, those things which are central to the Christian tradition (the cross, the resurrection, the Jewishness of Christ) remain central, yet because they are central they are not seen as being too brittle to face challenge and deep interrogation. It may be that some of those things that we have seen as central to the Christian faith do indeed fail under such a challenge, but if this does prove to be the case, then we might question their role in the faith in the first place.

This form of queering is perhaps best described as Catholic Queering – a commitment to the catholic faith, yet a commitment that does not fear for the collapse of that faith if questions are asked of it.[12] In many ways, churches have behaved in questions of sex and sexuality as though God is sitting scandalised at the other end of the table, and must be protected from conversations about anal

---

[12] Of course, it is impossibly simplistic to suggest that Protesting or Catholic queering is a binary choice, or that there is not significant overlap between the methods (and, indeed, the possible outcomes). What is being highlighted here is that the queering approach in this book takes place within a particular tradition, which suggests that there is something to reveal beneath the imprisoning graveclothes of normativity. All is up for challenge, but it is challengeable because of an overriding belief in the solidity of the foundations of the faith.

intercourse, sadomasochism, or casual sex. This is quite clearly a preposterous way to behave, yet as Christians we all too frequently seem willing to act in a way that suggests we need to protect our faith and our God from offence. The issue, of course, is that 'offence' is in the eye of the beholder, and the reality of God is not. God – and our faith – if they are real – must surely be able to cope with the reality of life. God – and our faith – can cope with our questions, our challenges, our frustrations, however tiresome they might be. God – and our faith – can cope with queering, and indeed our faith is enriched by it.

We shall see examples of this Catholic Queering found throughout this book and further described below. For now, it is worth raising one other objection to the endeavour of queering our faith – that of the risk of a triumph of intellectualism. Proponents of queer theology have not infrequently been accused of using more words than are necessary to ask a question, and rather a lot of technical language that makes the whole enterprise inaccessible. There is some truth in this allegation, although anti-intellectualism is rather a plague of the modern church, and valid concerns can rather too easily spill over into a widespread suspicion of critical scholarship. Yet to pose this particular concern simply, we might ask whether queer theologians are placing the intellect – or, to use the classical Anglican model, reason – above Scripture (and Tradition).

Beyond the inevitable confected howls of outrage that any challenge to well-beloved idols of the faith will inevitably procure, there is nonetheless a serious case to answer in this regard. The three-legged stool model, together with its Wesleyan gift of experience, is well known and was covered in some detail in *Queer Holiness*, and we won't cover that ground again here, except to note that a more helpful understanding of the role of Scripture, Tradition, Reason, and Experience, might be the use of the latter three as lenses through which to read the former (and, indeed, to read and challenge each other). The question then arises – if everything is up for debate, whither the role of Scripture (and, indeed, Tradition)?

It is, of course, a fundamental misunderstanding of the whole process of queering to suggest that everything is up for debate in precisely the same way. For some queer theologians (who, of course, become convenient bogeymen), that will indeed be the case, but for most there will be levels of nuance that need to be taken into account. To take Biblical interpretation as an example, we might already begin to notice the process of queering taking place – at least to some moderate and rather restricted degree – in the development of various forms of Biblical criticism and our greater willingness to pay attention to culture, context, intended and received meaning when we seek to understand the scriptures and their message for the world of today. Here, there is a challenge to the normative reading of scripture, a reading that has become 'orthodox' yet may well fly in the face of what the text actually says. It is fascinating that a number of evangelical scholars (and even bloggers) now take this way of engaging with scripture as read.

Of course, there is historical precedent for such a reading – from the Fathers to the modern day – and indeed it would be perverse to place a normative interpretation ahead of proper interpretative scholarship. Yet this is absolutely in the same channel as queering – albeit queering moves beyond any attempt at objectivity to ask questions of scripture from a positionality (or rather positionalities) that is itself non-normative. The willingness to ask questions of scripture – which may indeed include questions of the formation of the canon, and the weighing up of the ways that different scripture may speak to the contemporary world – is not a threat unless there are unspoken yet present questions of power and authority in interpretation, or fear that the texts cannot stand on their own and face such scrutiny. Our queering does not reject Scripture – it interrogates it, and in so doing, it strengthens it.

Turning to Tradition, there is perhaps more of a genuine threat from queering, yet such a threat will only be described as such by those who are wedded to the outward forms rather than the inward realities of what that Tradition embraces and passes on. Sacred Tradition is far too frequently associated with the outward, and with the peripheral, rather than with the actual faith received and handed on, in practices and beliefs. These practices, which will include sacramental practices, are important because of what they point to – that is, God – rather than because of any particular externality. Similarly, it is entirely possible that in the handing on of faith, the externalities receive more emphasis and ultimately become more important in the handing on than that which they point toward. We shall see in the following chapters how queering can actually strengthen this faith and its practices, rather than weaken it – how queering can help us grasp what is at the heart of what we believe, and ask deep questions about whether we truly embody that in what we do, and in what we say about what we believe, deepening our faith in and relationship with God. The faith is unchanging but the outward forms may be different in each generation – indeed, we know them to be so. It is interesting that in matters of sexuality, the church has been so resistant to this change – a comment, perhaps, on its insecurity in matters sexual, reflecting a church that is unable to ask the right questions for fear of the possible answers.

Reason is not, then, being placed above the other parts of that famous stool, but what is happening is a refusal to play the silly games that suggest 'the scriptures are really clear' on whatever topic of the moment that is being debated. The process of queering says, instead, that Scripture is quite capable of being challenged and engaged with from a variety of real-life perspectives, which may come in the form of reason or experience. That does not – categorically – make experience or reason the senior partner. Instead, it makes our grappling with scripture and tradition more serious, more careful, more genuine, and more life-giving. Within it are the seeds of fruitful dialogue, which need to be given the opportunity to see the light of day rather than be hacked down for fear of being too dangerous for the neatly mown lawn. The normative has been in control for far too long – now is the time to redress the balance.

THE THREADS OF QUEER

Let us return, then, to the different strands that make up queer theology. As we have said previously, there are not necessarily clear and set boundaries around what is and is not to be included in queer theology, but various theologians have made attempts to clarify what is meant by the field in general. Patrick Cheng has done so in a helpful and succinct way, and it is his definitions that we will make use of here. Noting that the sources of queer theology are queered forms of scripture, tradition, reason, and experience,[13] Cheng suggests three definitions (or strands) of queer theology.[14] The first of these is 'LGBT [sic] people "talking about God"', and we might add 'and talking about the created order and our place within it in the light of this talk about God'. The second is '"talking about God" in a self-consciously transgressive manner, especially in terms of challenging societal norms about sexuality and gender'. The third is '"talk about God" that challenges and deconstructs the natural [sic] binary categories of sexual and gender identity'.[15]

These three categories are frequently combined and intertwined, and you will find all three aspects within these pages. Of particular importance, however, is the intentional progression found moving from the first to the second and third of these forms of thought, something that is not universally accepted amongst LGBTQI Christians and their allies. There remains a temptation – an understandable one – to try to fit into the cis-heterosexual box, not least amongst those for whom

[13] Patrick Cheng, *Radical Love: An Introduction to Queer Theology* (New York: Seabury, 2011) p.xi
[14] Ibid p.9
[15] Ibid p.9

that state of normativity has been in some way unconsciously sanctified. It is thus entirely possible for LGBTQI Christians to talk about God without bridging the gap to the much more contentious aspects of queer theology, where normativity and its idols are threatened by queerness. It is understandable that some feel this is a step too far – understandable, but regrettable. It is perhaps because of this reluctance that we remain mired in conversations about same-sex marriage rather than spending time discussing what is at the heart of the debate in the first place – love, relationality, holiness. Suggesting that gay couples are 'just like straight couples' is a much easier argument to win. The problem is that the resulting lack of progress does a disservice to straight and gay alike.

To return to the four sources of queer theology that Patrick Cheng outlines, one of his key contentions is that scripture, tradition, reason and experience can each be queered and together form the wellspring from which queer theology – in its multiple forms – comes.[16] Again, there is no simple way to neatly divide these four sources – in the queer paradigm, each of these interacts and intersects with the other. Queer experience feeds into our queering of scripture; queer reason can similarly impact on how we understand tradition; and so on. Not only are these four the wellspring but this wellspring itself is constantly engaged with and changed, with queerness ultimately acting as an iterative and creative generator of new ideas and refinement of the old, feeding into a rich tapestry of thought that enables us to say both more about God, and to recognise when we should be surely saying less. To do queer theology is to do it queerly.

WHAT IS OUR QUEER APPROACH?

This all being said, we must now turn to the approach of this book – the way we intend to undertake the queering

---

[16]   Ibid pp.11-22

enterprise. As has been described above, this book will take a Catholic Queering approach, working from within the tradition to enrichen it. We will take the life, death and resurrection of Jesus Christ as revealed truth, and the tradition of the church as a rich fountain from which to draw. We will not, however, shy away from challenging the sources of Christian understanding and belief, and nor will we be content with a Christianity that settles into comfortable normativity rather than opening itself up to challenge.

A key starting point, too, is the existence of holy queer love and lives. We fundamentally reject the idea that queer people are especially morally deficient because of their queerness or its being lived out, and instead argue that their relating to others – platonically, romantically, sexually – should face similar questions to those who are not queer rather than be subject to an additional level of censure. Having engaged with reason and experience, we find non-cis-heterosexual interpersonal relating to be a normal variant of human behaviour. In other words, our starting point here is not cis-heteronormativity – it is, instead, a focus on the equal personhood of each individual, and a recognition that same-sex or same-gender love is in no consequential way different to that which our church calls normative. This is not, primarily, a book arguing for why that is the case – it is a book that engages with the reality of the world which shows it to be so. It rejects the normative in favour of engaging with the world that God has actually made.

In so doing, it also rejects the patriarchal and racist schemas that our societies and – quite often – our church have caused to develop, and brings us back to the fundamentals of our faith which have been so easily lost through Christian enculturation and power-seeking, institutionalisation and imperialism. It aims to reorient our theology and practice around the core of Christian doctrine and meaning, rather than seeking to prop up the peripheries at all costs. It seeks to do all this by refusing to take either societal norms or emphatically expressed binaries as Gospel truth – instead, its starting point is the diversity of human life, and the blessedness, holiness and God-givenness of this diversity. It rejects the age-old argument of assigning everything we cannot explain or do not like to doctrine of the Fall, and instead demands that we ask exactly what God is doing through the lives of those we, as a church, too often refuse to listen to. It calls for less directing, and more hearing.

In our next chapter, we will further tease out some of these themes. For now, an example of how this might work in practice seems in order. Let us consider a same-sex/same-gender relationship. The self-declared 'orthodox' Christian perspective would be to say such a thing is forbidden, or less-than, or at the very most should be somehow accommodated in a way so as to prevent disruption to the cis-heterosexual world view.The starting point here is baptised cis-heteronormativity. Our starting point is quite different – we reject the normative (however Christianised) as having any claim to moral authority or ethical precedence, and instead take the relationship as our starting point. We interrogate it – we ask whether such relationships show and build up virtue and reflect something of God. We take the evidence and listen to the voice of those on the margins of Christian 'decency'. We open ourselves up to the possibility that the Spirit is doing something beyond the bounds of normativity.

Yet it is not enough to merely see that the Spirit is doing something good, and then try to find ways of fitting such people into pre-defined culturally Christian categories, boxes that we have made by human design, often with the very best of intentions, yet boxes which are by their nature contingent and must be open to change. Instead, we must be willing to allow this new recognition to shape our Christian lives in their entirety – to change those boxes. Seeing the grace and love in a same-sex/same-gender relationship should not only move us to call such a thing marriage – if indeed that is the right term (and we shall return to this later in the book) – but it should also move us to interrogate the nature and meaning of marriage in the light of this. It should call us to a reassessment of what it is that marriage signifies rather than a focus merely on the peripherals of 'man and woman'. It should move us to ask much more interesting and important questions about human relating, and love, and the relationship with the divine. It should bring us to an enriched form of the faith which is of benefit to others, and which is founded on the holy diversity that God has created rather than the normativity we have succeeded in imposing.

Queer people and queer experience have much to say to the world, and to the church. Many of us are already saying and doing it. These pages will outline what some of the consequences might be if we were willing and able to break free of our servitude to normativity. Time will tell whether we have the courage to do so.

3

THE QUEER CHALLENGE

Facing things that don't sit easily with us, or that challenge our preconceptions about the world, is by its nature not a comfortable thing to do. For many people, Christians amongst them, it would simply be much easier if queer people didn't exist.[1] 'Conservative' bloggers and self-appointed moral arbiters speak carelessly of 'gender ideology' or of the 'queer agenda', hoping in the process to scare off enough good, law-abiding Christians and warn them away from dipping their toes in the dangerous, heresy-infested waters of LGBTQIA-affirming Christianity, or – even worse – queer theology. Such voices are often loud, and the truthfulness of their claims are often in direct opposition to the confidence with which they assert them.[2]

There are a variety of different ways to pursue that kind of thinking. One is to simply wish, and in some cases assert, that we didn't and don't exist. We're either mistaken or we're just a

[1]   This does not remain an abstract proposition in many parts of the world, and it is beyond scandalous that the Anglican Archbishop of Uganda used his Easter Day message to call for the incarceration (at minimum) of queer people rather than to focus on the resurrection of Jesus Christ. The reality is that queer people exist and the only 'problem' that there is with this comes from those who oppose them – if such prejudice did not exist, there would be no problem.

[2]   It is important to note quite how powerful this network can be – it is a well-funded and networked pan-church and pan-national attempt to erase queer people and queerness from the church and, often, society. Breakaway 'Anglican' groups are good examples of this – people whose 'Anglicanism' is defined in terms of opposition to queerness.

cultural phenomenon that will fade away as the world 'wakes up'.[3] Another might simply be to cast us all as so depraved, so evil, that we must be ignored or – better – punished.[4] We can be imbued with all kinds of evil intentions, or we can be cast as sexually incontinent, disturbed individuals whose 'intrinsic disorder' compromises any claim we might make to have our voices heard. Most pernicious of all is the relatively recent phenomenon of 'conservatives' who 'feel sorry' for us and our plight, and talk of pastoral accompaniment that at best involves telling us not to have sex and instead offer up our desires as sacrificial suffering, and at worst invokes some kind of conversion 'therapy' [sic].

All of these have a single aim, which is to ensure that the insights and challenges that come with queerness do not impinge upon, let alone influence, the comfortable patriarchal cis-heteronormative framework that Christianity has settled itself into over the past two millennia. The intentions for such an aim might be varied, but are frequently driven by some kind of fear, whether temporal or eschatological. A threat to the church's comfortable self-understanding is never welcome, and it seems that it is most particularly unwelcome when so much of church culture is built on a silent queerness.

Queerness is nothing new for the church, as we shall see when we more fully interrogate the different ways that queerness can be applied to institutions. Yet it is fascinating that for a church that in many ways is (or rather should be) by its nature in opposition to the prevailing cultural norms of patriarchal cis-heteronormativity, nonetheless so much of wider church culture seems to be desperate to prove itself in such terms. The church seems almost ashamed of its lack of

[3] We see this in recent attempts to reduce queerness to 'ideology', where an individual is then dehumanised and reduced to a 'problem'.
[4] Yet the language is often that of 'discipline' rather than punishment. Discipline can then be used to protect the moral majority from the depravity of the queers – it is needed in order to ensure the pure church does not suffer insult or injury.

concordance with modern secular culture – those elements that appear too 'weird' or mystical are routinely rooted out in the name of some vague notion of 'accessibility'. Whilst in recent years in the West an opposition to same-sex or gender relationships has frequently been posited as a countercultural positioning, this is a crass oversimplification, and ignores huge swathes of cultural conditioning that has impacted the church over the past several hundred years, and indeed continues to do so. The Church of England's way of relating to homosexuality, in particular, is absolutely of its culture and context, albeit a culture and a context of several years ago.

Queering Christianity, then, is not a new enterprise – in fact, it gives Christians an opportunity to rediscover much of what Christianity is, freed from the cultural lens that plagues so much of Western Christianity. Of course, the association with the West is in itself a problem for Christianity's own self-understanding – many theological treatises are written, sermons preached, and seminary educations undertaken without a single reference to the birthplace of Christianity, its African early history, or its world-wide nature. Far too often, Christianity becomes a plaything of the rich western world.

ISSUES OF CULTURE

This reality brings us back to the question posed at the end of the first chapter: so is this all just about gay, White middle-class men getting married? In the context of the Church of England, and indeed in the more progressive parts of the Anglican Communion, this does appear to be a fair challenge. Many of the voices are gay men, many of the voices are White, many of the voices are middle-class – on both sides of this 'debate'. That is, of course, not uniformly the case, but given the cultural context of Whiteness and patriarchy, it is inevitably those voices which are given the greatest cultural amplification (and which have access to exercise their voices in the first place). It is worth our asking whether what we are attempting here will truly change the playing field, or rather whether it will simply move the dial from one group of White, middle-class men to another group of White, middle-class men, whilst in the process making very little difference to anyone else.

One of the key contentions of queerness is that this cannot be allowed to happen under any circumstances. It is perhaps this that proves so painful to many who don't want the infection of queerness to destroy the comfortable church – and for those of us who are White, middle-class gay men, is something which we must be reminded of time and time again. For many of us, it would be easier to simply slot into the cis-heterosexualist narrative, albeit as homosexuals, and this has certainly been the way that some activists, campaigners and even theologians have chosen. There is an attraction to being included on others' terms, but this is not the work of queer theology and nor, we might argue, does it do justice to the potential found within the Christian Gospel. If we believe something, we are surely obliged to let it out, however fearful that might make us.

We need to recognise quite how fundamental a shift this will be for us individually, but also for a church more widely. In the secular world, it is by no means clear that all LGBTQIA people would see themselves as part of a wider movement, with responsibilities to others who are not like themselves. In *Queer Holiness*, we discussed the importance of intersectionality, and here we need to make this clear once again. If we allow our queering to be pedestrianised, to become another tool of Whiteness or classism or patriarchy or misogyny or ableism, or any of the elements of structural oppression that continue to plague the church and the world, then we will have fundamentally failed in our duty – and indeed in our stated aim. This book is written by a White, middle class, gay man from Europe, and hence cannot begin to properly embody the complexity of the world-wide queer experience, with the various forms of traumatisation and ostracisation, solidarity and self-conception. We must surely be open to hearing the voices of those who are not heard and allow them to challenge our own preconceptions – whether queer or otherwise.

It is for this reason, for example, that a simplistic acceptance of pernicious narratives of 'conservative global south' vs 'progressive west' are so dangerous in ecclesial conversations about sexuality and gender. Far too often, we are presented with this as a *fait accompli* – that Black Africans, for example, are uniformly opposed to same-sex relationships whereas the white liberal church in the United States is uniformly in favour. This is demonstrably untrue, and our unwillingness to challenge this narrative means that queer Black Christians the world over, in our own context and in the global south, are forgotten, ignored, or erased. We do ourselves a huge disservice when we do not interrogate these statements more fully, and when we do not consider the dynamics at play in statements that come from some of the more conservative churches.

We similarly perpetuate a racist narrative when we accept the idea that being opposed to LGBTQIA rights is inherently countercultural (or, indeed, countercultural in a straightforwardly Biblical sense). It is not – it is, rather, countercultural to some parts of white western culture. Yet we know that this is not the only culture that exists in the white western world, let alone more generally, and it is an act of staggering racism when we see being countercultural only in relation to one particular form of white, western culture, and link this countercultural attitude with Biblical approval. We hold responsibility as Christians to name this, and refuse to allow political arguments to be built on the back of queer Black Africans. Similarly, we hold responsibility to name the complex dynamics that led to the development of different cultural biases globally, not least the racist colonial attitudes and behaviours of white western nations, and the complex dynamics that have led to modern conceptions of queer equality in some societies. Finally, we do no justice to the Biblical text by presenting a simplistic understanding of the context and nature of, and impetus for, countercultural narratives in scripture.

Refusing to engage only in questions of marriage, and refusing to engage in questions solely through one particular lens, means that we commit to doing much more than simply finding a way to fit LGBTQIA people into the church. Our business, instead, is to put a stumbling block in the way of the *status quo*, not because there is necessarily something wrong with everything the church has inherited – far from it – but because we have, on occasion, consciously or unconsciously ossified culture to become a church-shaped idol. There is nothing inherently patriarchal, for example, about Christianity – but there does seem to be something inherently patriarchal about the church. These two things sit uncomfortably with one another, and cry out for some work to be done. In so doing, we may well end up with many of the things that we had before, but these will be tried and tested in the face of reality, and in the process we will learn and understand more about who and what we are as Christians, and what it is that we are trying to say about God and about the world.

QUEER OTHERING

It is a natural human reaction to 'other' people different to ourselves. In the context of conversations about sexuality and gender, an easy method of othering is turning people into abstractions. In so doing, we can convert people into who they are 'for us' rather than who they are themselves. Even the most well-meaning of allies can fall into this trap – and, indeed, the term ally itself is a loaded one, suggesting that the people with the problem are the oppressed group themselves. This is fundamentally not true – the sickness lies in the way society and the church engages with 'the other'.[5] In church discussions of queer people, it is so vanishingly

[5] I am grateful to Dr Elizabeth Henry for her insights here, which she explores in Episode 3 of the 'What is Justice?' podcast hosted by St John the Divine, Kennington, in 2022 (available here: https://open.spotify.com/episode/6ChnP62Vu4qm1IwzL1KDoJ [accessed October 7th 2023]

rare to find ourselves described as anything else than 'other' that we might be forgiven for believing it.

Alan Wilson, one of the few bishops in the Church of England who has been consistently willing to stand up for LGBTQI people whatever the personal cost, has succinctly described this reality, stating that 'discriminatory attitudes are everyone's problem ... a society that tolerates discrimination diminishes itself, not only the people against whom it is directed'.[6] Such discrimination and othering can be very subtle indeed. He quotes the educator Jane Elliott whose research calls into question the 'nobility' of those who say 'they [do] not see other people as black [in this particular example, although the same might be said of queer people] but simply as people'. For all that this sounds on the surface to be a process of anti-othering, in fact it tries to turn queers into honorary non-queers and is a subtle yet dangerous power play that states 'I do not see you as you are. I want to see you as I would be more comfortable seeing you'.[7] Queer people in the church, therefore, face the blunt othering in which they are set beyond the pale, seen and described as somehow aberrant, outside the church and inherently destructive, yet they also face this more pernicious and yet equally dangerous othering of erasure, in which they are tolerated only on others' terms. Their distinctiveness is either dangerous or non-existent – neither of which grows a healthy church.

The drive towards queer non-existence may well be unconscious and – at least on the face of it – well intentioned, albeit showing an extraordinary inability and unwillingness to face up to the inherent power dynamics in an institution like the church. Yet this form of erasure has a more sinister cousin, normalisation. This normalisation is anything but a neutral

6 Alan Wilson, *More Perfect Union?: Understanding Same-sex Marriage* (London: Darton, Longman and Todd, 2014) p.48
7 Jane Elliott, *The Angry Eye – All in One*, 2000, video, as quoted in Alan Wilson, *More Perfect Union?: Understanding Same-sex Marriage* (London: Darton, Longman and Todd, 2014) p.48

process, and is rather a bare-faced expression of privilege and power. Martín Hugo Córdova Quero describes this process of normalisation as being 'labelling, dehumanising, demonising, exoticising, stigmatising, and silencing',[8] a process which benefits from the construction of and then enforcement of binaries into which individuals must fit.[9] We will return to these binaries below.

The even simpler trope of the queer as being an unbeliever outside the church is one that is relied upon by opponents of LGBTQI inclusion both consciously and unconsciously. The use of Romans 1 to oppose LGBTQI inclusion, in fact, relies upon the idea of non-cis-heterosexual intimacy being a signifier of rebellion against God. Putting aside the complexity, audience and intention of the text, and its translation, for one moment, what is particularly interesting is the way that this text is treated by those whose ideology rejects queer holiness. The argument from this passage is often presented as though what Paul is doing is listing a group of forbidden actions – but this is not the meaning or purpose of the passage. Instead, the 'vice list' is actually a list of actions that have occurred as a result of the lack of honour and thanksgiving given to God (Romans 1:22). It hinges on the 'therefore' in verse 24, and the 'for this reason' in verse 26 – and the vices contained in verse 27 – are a **result** of this turning away from God.[10]

To use this passage to oppose same-sex/same-gender intimacy requires us, therefore, to accept that such intimacy is a **result** of turning away from God. The

---

[8] Martín Hugo Córdova Quero, 'The Prostitutes Also Go into the Kingdom of God: A Queer Reading of Mary of Magdala' in Marcella Althaus-Reid, ed., *Liberation Theology and Sexuality* (Aldershot: Ashgate, 2006) pp.81-82
[9] Ibid p.98
[10] Note that this is an *active, intentional* turning away from God (see Romans 1:18-23), and hence cannot be neatly assigned to The Fall as though it is merely an expression of transmitted original sin (itself a very confusing idea, as it is not at all clear why particular people should express this particular form of 'sin' (disordered affections) whilst others get off scot-free.

'shameless acts' described are a result of this turning away in the same way as being 'filled with every kind of injustice, evil, covetousness, malice' is. Because this intimacy is a **result** of the turning away, it is a sign but not the cause of the rebellion – it is something people end up doing because they have first turned away from God. Thus, whether we accept or do not accept that our contemporary understanding of same-sex/same-gender intimacy is indeed included within this 'vice list' (which we should not), the only logical way that this passage can be used to oppose same-sex and gender intimacy is by arguing that those who are attracted to those of the same sex or gender find such attraction because of a prior rejection of and rebellion against God.

This is an absurd argument, but given the heavy reliance on this passage by those who oppose LGBTQI relationships, it points to an inherent belief that LGBTQI people are in a very real sense 'other', because they are in active rebellion against God, and that before they start anything in the bedroom. This may help to explain the suspicion and fear shown by some of the most conservative Christians towards LGBTQI people, and whilst much is made of 'hate the sin, love the sinner', and the more subtle 'it's the acts that are sinful, not the orientation', it is hard to see how this can be reconciled with the clear meaning of the Romans text. If we are to use Paul's argument to condemn LGBTQI people, we must surely condemn the orientation as well – the orientation being a 'desire' of 'hearts to impurity' (Romans 1:24) which itself is a result of wilful rebellion against God. Yet, of course, we know this – by experience, and by reason – not to be the case.

We have previously mentioned the evils of the psychological trauma that is given the misnomer of 'conversion therapy' previously, yet beyond a very niche group of Christian protagonists, the idea that sexual orientation can be changed by will (and by force) has been shown to be nonsense, and all reputable psychological and psychiatric organisations fundamentally reject the premise.[11] To put this another way, we know by reason (and experience) that being attracted to someone of the same sex or gender is not something that can be changed, and is not a choice. In other words, it is not wilful rebellion. This poses a very real challenge to the use of Romans 1 as a text that has anything to say whatsoever about same-sex or same-gender attraction or orientation, or indeed 'acts' (a dreadful term). This is not casuistry – it is sincere engagement with the text.

BEYOND 'INCLUSION'

Once we take the rather pedestrian and yet still contested step to say that LGBTQI people who profess Christ are not outside the church, and are not unbelievers, then we are also compelled to leave talk of 'inclusion'. LGBTQI people do not need to be included in anything, and indeed the suggestion that they do is itself simply a reiteration of the cis-heteronormativity that continues to lord it over our church institutions. As Alan Wilson says, 'there is a fundamental problem about saying you love someone but reserve the right to sit in judgement over them'.[12] Yet to fully appreciate this is to recognise that the very nature of the church itself changes. For LGBTQI people to be included in God's church by God in the same way that anyone else is, means that listening to queer Christian experience is an essential part of getting to know all that God is doing in God's church. Queer experience is not second best or a fringe issue – it's front and centre. The same, of course, is true of the experience of many others who have historically been marginalised in the church – women, Black people and other people of colour, disabled people – the list goes on. None of these are to be included in

---

[11] The Royal College of Psychiatrists, the Royal College of General Practitioners, the UK Council for Psychotherapy, NHS England, the American Psychological Association, to name a few.

[12] Alan Wilson, *More Perfect Union?: Understanding Same-sex Marriage*, p. 49.

the church – all of them are already a vital and integral part of the church. It is the human institution that needs to catch up with this reality – and rather than find ways to 'include' LGBTQI people in second-best institutions like civil partnerships, the church needs to be open to being genuinely challenged by them as fellow Christians.

Of course, we have seen historically what happens when the reality of this begins to sink into those who currently hold the power. The violent opposition in the corridors of power to the Liberation Theologies of the late twentieth century show exactly what happens when the liberation of the oppressed risks the power of the oppressors. Of course, a recurring theme that we have seen is that the liberation of an oppressed group will benefit the whole and not solely that group, but it is inevitable that there will be perceived 'losers' in any such triumph, most particularly if those in power seek to hold onto it by nefarious means. The continued hold of cis-heteronormativity (as a social norm) over the Church of England is seen in the outright refusal of a number of gay bishops to come out, the refusal of anyone in authority to even use the word 'queer', and the ongoing refusal to recognise that the lack of queer representation in the House or College of Bishops is a damning indictment on our church. As one diocesan bishop is reported to have said at a meeting of clergy, 'well, the gay clergy can always become Deans'. That this comment came after – rather than before – the Church of England's most recent foray into 'inclusion' (the Living in Love and Faith project) speaks volumes about the extremely limited impact such a project has had.

Were the leaders and powerholders (both official and unofficial) in the church to be more open to the challenge that queer identity being integral to the church embodies, then they might find themselves surprised and delighted by the enrichment that it could bring. As Karen Keen points out, 'discerning the divine meaning of Scripture requires distinguishing the inspired message from the temporal, cultural mode of delivery', otherwise we risk assuming that 'the biblical authors' *accent* is divine'.[13] This discernment is fundamentally more fruitful when all the voices of the church are heard, and not only those given sanction by the self-appointed arbiters.[14] By excluding those whom God has included, we fail to live up to the task of interpretation that is gifted to us, and risk placing our emphasis in the wrong place. Queer experience is part of Christian experience, and we need it to properly inhabit our lives in the church corporate.

WIDENING OUR HORIZONS

Queering the church, its institutions, theology, doctrines, practice, and mission, is no easy task. As we have seen – and consistently see in public debates – the willingness of the wider church to permit such an enterprise is extremely limited. In 'progressive' parts of the Anglican Communion, it is by no means clear that such a queering has actually taken place. Debates remain far too often within the confines of normativity, and in the words of Linn Tonstad 'as a search for the permitted and the forbidden ... about finding ways to move (mostly monogamous, married) same-sex relationship from the column of sexual acts marked "illicit" (forbidden) to the column marked "licit" (permitted)'.[15] We therefore fail to move beyond discussions of what goes where, when, and how, towards a place where the underlying philosophical and theological questions are asked.

As has been mentioned, whilst we must surely give thanks that churches such as The Episcopal Church in the United States now permit same-sex/same-gender marriage, this is not the same as that church having undertaken a proper process of queering. Our determination to think in

---

[13] Karen Keen, *Scripture, Ethics & The Possibility of Same-Sex Relationships* (Grand Rapids, MI: Eerdmans, 2018) p.45
[14] Matthew 11:25 springs to mind.
[15] Linn Tonstad, *Queer Theology* p.4

categorical terms seems to be hardwired into our (particularly western) way of undertaking the theological (and the wider academic) enterprise.[16] A true process of queering can free us from engaging in questions in this way, and instead enable us to approach things – and people – as they are, rather than give in to our apparent *felt* need to categorise them (often in simplistic binaries) before doing so.

In the previous chapter, we met Patrick Cheng's three streams of queer theology, and we noted his use of the word 'natural' when describing 'binary categories of sexual and gender identity'. It is worth our returning to that challenge here. We must be extremely careful when we interpret what Cheng means by 'natural'. As he develops his ideas, Cheng importantly notes a distinction between those categories that are societally (and we might add ecclesially, culturally, and everything in between) constructed and imposed, and those which appear to have some grounding in 'nature' – those we might call 'biologically essentialist'. As he identifies, this distinction is helpful to some degree, but runs the risk of overly privileging particular processes of categorisation that we call 'biological'. In other words, 'natural' is itself a loaded term, and we must be careful in our definition of it.

'Natural' may be viewed as a biological or a theological term, and there is no clear reason why these two should entirely align. To give an example, we might ask why it is that we see sex as an important theological category. Sex is an important biological category to some degree, although it is not simply binary (as a simple understanding of the role of sex across the animal kingdom, let alone plant and other kingdoms, will show, and the fact of intersexuality within normal human variation). Sex has been adopted as an important theological natural category, not least in recent attempts to use the Genesis narrative to impose a gender and sex essentialism on theological anthropology. Yet queer

[16]   An interesting parallel is the continued reliance on categorical diagnoses in psychiatric manuals (although this is currently a situation in flux).

experience and reason demands we question whether this essentialism and categorisation is actually theologically important. Does the male-ness and female-ness, and the express refusal to acknowledge anything else-ness, matter in a fundamental, theological, way? Are our differences ontologically important, and if so, why? If not, why are we determined to hold onto our binaries?

This matter becomes more complicated when we consider ideas of gender. Whilst there has been what appears to be an intentional muddying of the waters on questions of sex and gender by those who are ideologically opposed to challenging complementarian theological narratives, it is abundantly clear that sex and gender are distinct, and that the latter falls far more into Cheng's concept of the societally determined than the 'natural'. The same questions that we ask above about sex might rightly be applied to gender – and yet when we are willing to view gender as a social construct, we similarly must ask further questions of sex. Turning to the endlessly frustrating (and banal) arguments around women's ministry, which category is it that opponents of women priests are using to determine their 'impossibility' – it is sex, or gender? In other words, are we talking about the presence or absence of sex organs and physiology (and if so, which – gonadal, secondary – and what counts as an absence – total, or partial) or are we arguing about gender identity? What about someone who has XY chromosomes and male gonads, and yet has undeveloped secondary somatic sexual characteristics and has been 'brought up' as a woman (by gender)? Should this person be ordained?

The classic argument made in such cases is that these exceptions do not really matter or impact on the wider theological point, which is that *in most cases* sexual facets (and their cultural gender associations) align, and that – in essence – people in whom this does not happen are an anomaly and can be comfortably ignored. Not only is this pastorally grotesque, but it also fails to recognise the import of the initial question. If we are saying that gender or sex are theologically natural categories – that they have theological and ontological meaning – then we cannot neatly dodge this debate without surrendering our theological integrity. Queer experience means we cannot simply ignore these questions. Queering our faith hence means we need to pay attention to reality.

QUEERNESS AS A GIFT TO THE CHURCH

Our contention here is, ultimately, that queerness makes more sense of Christianity than its lack. It is not some bizarre and weird aberration – it is part and parcel of the Christian life. Queering is not about inclusion – and the risk with inclusion is that in our desire to bring people 'in', we surreptitiously and often unconsciously replace Christ as the Head of the Church. In so doing, we end up forgetting which people to include and focusing on an erasure of differences, differences which should be a gift and not an inconvenience. Our worship of the normative is not merely a refusal to recognise and embrace queer lives, but is wrapped up in a wider refusal to privilege anything beyond the cis-heteronormative, male, able-bodied, wealthy, White western class that has ruled the church officially and unofficially for generations. Indeed, our acceptance that normalcy exists – that normativity is valid as a theological category – is little more than a blasphemous attempt to replace God-given diversity with comfortable human categories.

Yet we are in such a place because of the success of cis-heterosexuality as ideology,[17] as 'theology, as normative

---

[17] We shall engage with this further in later chapters. It may appear strange to refer to heterosexuality as an ideology, but the question arises as to whether there is truly something *categorical* in heterosexuality (opposite to homosexuality) or whether the whole idea of this being a separate category is itself ideological.

sociopolitical and, crucially, economic system'.[18] In Tonstad's words:

> 'heterosexuality as a system doesn't deal with truth. Theological heterosexuality deals with fictions, ideas of what human beings ought to be like that are divorced and distanced from the reality of human, bodied, sexual life. Yet these fictions get used against people.'

Tonstad goes onto make the explicit link between cis-heterosexualism as a system that oppresses the poor as well as the queer – a recognition central to the findings of queer theology. Cis-heterosexualism is much more than the policing of sex and gender – although it is indeed that too. It is a way of life that plays on the desire for respectability, for 'fitting in', for 'striving', and for all kinds of other ways of judging the utility or worth of others' lives that, ways that when properly examined theologically, have nothing of God in them. Cis-heterosexualism is ultimately a secular ideology imposed – willingly – on the sacred realm – an ideology that relies on its ability to shape wider cultural forms of meaning, status, and identity. Of course, until recent times the idea of homosexuality and heterosexuality were unknown, suggesting even more that the triumph of this ideology is a matter of concern rather than for celebration by theologians.

CONCLUSION

As we move towards engaging with our particular strand of queer theology in the matters of church doctrine and practice, including but not solely in ideas around sex and gender, let us return again to our argument made in our first chapter – the time for apologetics is well and truly over. Nothing of what has been written here will be engaged with

[18]   Linn Tonstad, *Queer Theology* p.76

by those who have bought into the ideology and idolatry of cis-heterosexualism and cis-heteronormativity. The dialogue, in that sense, is exhausted. There is much more to learn and discover for queer individuals and for their individual and collective reality within the church, but there is little that can be done with stopped ears, closed eyes and defensive egos.

Our task, then, is to meet people primarily as three-dimensional individuals – individuals within a community who have much to contribute to that community's self-understanding, if only that community would be willing to open itself to those gifts. In *Queer Holiness* we thought about Biblical hermeneutics – about how we might interpret the Bible in the light of queer experience and queer reality. Here, we must cast that net even further, and ask what this queer experience and reality might do to Christianity *tout court*. We are interested, then, not only in matters of interpretation, but also in our epistemology – our way of knowing. We will not only ask questions, but also ask whether those are the right questions to be asking. We will say an emphatic 'no' to the idea that the Texts of Terror[19] contain an easy-read set of answers to the pedestrian question of queer inclusion, and instead ask what the church might look like if we were willing to truly embody reality. It is to that task that we now turn.

---

[19] A term coined by Phyllis Trible – for further reading, see Phyllis Trible, *Texts of Terror: Literary-feminist Readings of Biblical Narratives* (Minneapolis, MN: Fortress, 1984).

PART II
QUEERING
OUR LOVES

4

QUEERING ... RELATIONSHIP

As we have discussed, queering is not only about LGBTQI people, and nor is it only about sex, sexuality, and gender. In many ways, a sole focus on these few topics when the church has spoken out on queer issues has belied the institutional church's failure (intentional or unintentional) to recognise that queer people might have something theological to say to, about, and from within the church. It is much easier to imagine that we are just disordered cis-heterosexuals, with a few issues that need 'pastoral accommodation' – a well-meaning yet rather slimy term. A focus on our sex lives as a problem needing to be solved is an easy way to ensure that the conversation remains on cis-heteronormative terms and that we remain within the bounds of 'inclusion'.

We shall explore some of this wider learning for the church as we walk through the latter part of this section. However, to begin with we will indeed engage with those matters of sex, sexuality, and gender, but from our own starting point and on our own terms. We will not buy into the narrative that we are somehow aberrant or bizarre, unnatural (that term again), or in need of being tamed. We will start, instead, by naming what is, by a focus on the reality that queer theology is ultimately all about. We will start by naming an unambiguous truth: our relationships, our loves, our lives, our desires, our embodied existence – all of these – are just as holy and God given and God beloved and God infused as anyone else's. There is no such thing as normal when it comes to sex, sexuality, and gender, and there is no such thing as normal because it is a theologically useless term. Indeed, the only thing that is normal – or rather, the only thing that 'is' – is the diversity of human experience which God has gifted us.

There is nothing wrong with us, as queers, more than there is with anyone else. *Contra* the Catechism of the Roman Catholic Church (and its various manifestations elsewhere),[1] we are not intrinsically disordered. We reject the Cartesian dualism of mind and body; we reject the Gnosticism that creeps into the church's discussions of sex and sexuality; we reject the idea that we need be measured against the cis-heteronormative ideal. We're here, we're queer, and God is working God's purpose out through us just as much as through anyone else. That being the case, the church needs to sit up and listen, because the lazy stereotypes and theological thinking that come about when the cis-heteronormative is given precedence are going to be smashed – and they need to be, because they're not up to the job. God's good creation includes us – on exactly the same terms as anyone else. Far from abstracting our lives and desires, the church is called to find ways of grappling with how and why God calls us into being part of God's church, too.

It is somewhat sad that these truths need to be spoken, yet if we are honest there are even some, perhaps many, of us – queer Christians – who sometimes find them hard to believe. We have been so conditioned by the church to see ourselves as a problem, as 'other', so conditioned to accept our role as a political football in endless debates about church 'unity', we have been so conditioned to think there just must be something wrong with us, that we have, to some degree, started to believe it. We have been all too willing to accept the scraps from under the table – we have been all too willing to do as we're told whilst the church

[1] Catechism of the Catholic Church, paragraph 2357, available here: https://www.vatican.va/archive/ENG0015/_INDEX.HTM [accessed October 7th 2023]

corporate does little more than spit in our faces. Our ability, our willingness, even, to accept and absorb the crass and virulent queerphobia of church policy and practice, our willingness to call something theological without seriously reflecting on the cultural bidirectionality, our willingness as queer Christians on occasion to acquiesce and calm the hearts and minds of those in authority – all of this is heaped upon our heads. It may come from a place of felt necessity, and indeed a place of trauma, but at some point, enough has to be enough.

When we – wounded by yet another attack – dare to lash out, however gently, we are reproached, told to speak 'more kindly', and gaslighted. When our lives are put up for discussion, we are expected to sit in rooms listening to the voices of others who say we are disordered and our relationships are worth nothing, engage 'appropriately', and smile sweetly over coffee. We are endlessly put on the defensive – endlessly pushed into apologetics, into feeling awkward for making everyone else's lives so difficult. The psychological abuse we face, and trauma that we then carry, is entirely ignored by the institutional church – a church that all-too-often lays the blame at our door. We are encouraged to rejoice in being part of a church that includes those 'with whom we disagree' – the very people who are telling our children, our young people, our vulnerable, that their very normal lives and loves are abnormal, sinful, hateful, wrong, ungodly. All of this done with a sickly smile and the ever-present threat of disciplinary action being taken against us. Well, enough is enough.

So in these pages, we have absolutely no intention of buying into that narrative. Queer goodness and holiness is our starting point, and from it we will ask what we might learn, as Christians – and someday, perhaps, as the church – about relationships, about sex, about marriage. The joy, the goodness, the holiness that seeps out of our relationships is a gift of God – a gift that enriches our own lives and the lives of those who we meet. God is ahead of us on all this – as ever!

Now is the time to truly believe that God is blessing us and take the leap of faith into all that this might reveal.

RELATIONSHIP AS REFLECTION

What exactly is relationship?

This is surely the question at the heart of who we are as human beings. Throughout what appears to be the entirety of human existence, human beings have had a need for relationship – for relating to and with other people, whether that be associates, friends, family, intimates, lovers. Each human society builds its own rules for the management of these relationships, and yet there is precious little evidence that we can do without this most basic of human behaviours. We appear – sociologically, neurologically, psychologically, anthropologically – built for relationship.

Yet this is not a merely secular enterprise – we know that our need for relationship is deeply theological as well. This need is not in some way an appendix to our life in Christ – it is central to it. Yet our contemporary Christian narrative so often adds an extra 's' onto the end of that word, and in so doing reduces all that the Christian story has to say about how we relate to one another into conversations about intimate partner relationships. Now it is certainly the case that the Christian faith does have something to say about such relationships, yet it surely has something to say there solely because of its having something to say about relationship in the first place – and, we might argue, it only has something to say about relationship because it has something to say about God.

The Biblical record is many things, but one of those is surely an account of the love story between God and God's people – a love story that is so often one-sided, and yet a love story that tells us much about the nature and the heart of God. By interrogating the relationship which sits at the heart of God, the Trinity, and the relationship of God with

God's people, we get a glimpse of the divine, grace-filled reality that infuses the universe and enlivens our hearts. We see longing in God's love – love that is projected *towards*. Yet this *towardsness* entails free choice – both for the lover and the beloved. Indeed, that free choice of *towarded* love surely tells us something of the nature of God, and hence of reality. Indeed, in looking upon the love of God for God's creation, we learn primarily about God – and from that, we learn about who we are called to be.

We might remind ourselves at this point that queerness is an intentional calling to mind of that reality. In other words, queerness should be – by its nature – demanding that our attention is focused on reality, disrupting the human lenses that we unintentionally place on our gaze and mistake for the reality that they distort. One of the ways that we end up doing this is in our failure to appropriately use metaphor in our discussion of God's love for God's people being like a marriage, or rather, where marriage imagery is used in a metaphorical way when speaking of God's love for God's people. The 'thing itself' is God's love, not marriage – marriage imagery is a tool to help us try to conceptualise what is being spoken of. Unfortunately, this subtlety has been all but lost in much contemporary preaching.

God's love for God's people is not – emphatically not – a marriage. Conversely, a marriage (whatever the sex or gender of the participants) is not – emphatically not – the same as God's love for God's people. It never can be and never has been, however helpful the metaphorical language may (or may not) be. Yet the elision of these two quite separate things has become so commonplace in contemporary preaching that we have lost sight of what the Biblical passages are trying to say in the first place.

The first thing that needs to be reiterated time and time again is that there is no such thing as 'marriage' – or rather, there is no single, timeless definition. When we read descriptions of marriage in the Old or New Testaments, we need to be endlessly alert to the role of culture and meaning each time the institution is mentioned, because its use in metaphor does not have a static meaning or purpose.

There remains a reticence to engage with Paul's writing, in particular, in this way. Adela Yarbro Collins highlights, through an engagement with feminist and womanist theology, the need to move beyond questions of intention towards a critical approach:

> 'It is not enough to determine what Paul said or meant in his ethical discourse ... some of the most basic images, values, and types of ethical reasoning in Paul's letters express relations amongst human beings that involve subordination and dominance. A simple transfer of such language to our own cultural context is dangerous for human flourishing.'[2]

She goes on to state that 'feminist and womanist criticism and hermeneutics originated to advocate the flourishing of White and Black woman. They have a broader relevance, however, for anyone who has suffered discrimination on the basis of religion, ethnicity, gender identity, or sexual orientation.' There is much here for us to muse on and be encouraged by – yet it surely takes courage, given the state of so much church dialogue on these disputed matters, to engage with Paul in this way. As she argues earlier in her paper, 'the key is "love" as an ethical norm'. We remain, it seems, ensnared by Paul's application of this norm (itself limited and contextualised) rather than the norm itself, and in so doing, lose sight of the primacy of love.

The second thing we must surely do is remind ourselves that our human relationships are not ever going to embody the fullness of the relationship that we learn about in holy scripture. They may indeed act as a foreshadowing of this relationship, or rather they may within them express and

---

[2] Adela Yarbro Collins, 'Ethics in Paul and Paul in Ethics', *Journal of Biblical Literature* Vol 142:1 (2023) pp.6-21

exemplify some of the key elements of the call to relationship that is at the heart of the universe, but they will never reach its fulness. We know this in particular to be the case when we consider the time-limited nature of marriage – marriage being a human institution that may indeed prepare us for holiness and yet which is not the end of any human life according to Our Lord's own teaching.

Thus, whilst marriage might indeed be a form of relationship which God can use to tell us something of reality, and indeed may be a form of relationship through which God can reveal God's love in a particular way, it is no more than that in its own relationship to that reality. The essence of marriage that matters when we make use of it to understand God's love in metaphorical terms is relationship. Everything else is peripheral, because everything else involved in 'marriage' is humanly derived and holds little value in the metaphorical endeavour. It is relationship which embodies and enshrines love, that builds on love, that springs from love. It is here that God might be glimpsed.

Indeed, our understanding of marriage has developed since that found in either the Old or New Testaments, and this understanding has emphasised different ways of thinking about relationship that have themselves adopted or rejected differing cultural norms. It is interesting to note that one of the key elements of marriage which remains in English law (and elsewhere) is its covenantal nature – the forming of a marriage through the exchange of vows rather than through the signing of a contract. This vowed exchange is absent from Civil Partnerships, and it is for this reason that the opening up of marriage to people of the same sex or gender is so important.

This covenantal understanding of marriage in a Christian context speaks ultimately of love and of freedom of choice. We must be absolutely clear that whilst this is our current understanding of covenant, and indeed may be reasonably assumed to form part of the essential nature of covenant, this understanding is something that has developed over time (in the main) to speak of radical equality between the couple. There remain churches who are committed to a 'Biblical' understanding of marriage which deny this equality, choosing to emphasise the culturally derived understandings of marriage found in the scriptures rather than to properly interrogate what is theological and what is cultural remnant. It is here that we see the ultimate power of cis-heteronormativity – a power to replace things of God with things of man, to disastrous effect.

CIS-HETERONORMATIVITY AS PERVASIVE PROJECT

We spoke of the Texts of Terror in the previous chapter. Whereas references to Old Testament texts (we might think of Leviticus 18:22) are today more frequently engaged with cautiously and with at least cursory attention given to the cultural context of what is written, it remains stunning that there appears to be a total unwillingness to do so when it comes to the New Testament, and in particular the Epistles. We continue to pluck verses out of them and use them as our 'Biblical' injunctions when it comes to sexuality and relationships. Using texts in this way is intellectually incoherent.

Yet we must take a step back and ask ourselves why it is that such a method – itself, incidentally, ahistorical – has such a prominent place in the church's current way of doing business. Or, perhaps, we might ask what it is that such a method enables, and how it benefits those with power. Here, things become rather clearer. Phrases such as 'the Bible has nothing positive to say about same-sex relationships' comes from the mouths of those who have already pre-determined that there is something particular, and ontologically different, about cis-heteronormative relationships and other relationships. Their hermeneutic derives from their ideology, and not the other way around.

All this suggests that the questions we have been asking

of scripture have themselves been wrong, because they are generated by those who have already made a distinction which itself is an interpretative choice or – at the very least – a positionality. If we refuse that false distinction, then our entire hermeneutics change. We approach the scriptures, instead, by asking what they have to say about covenant, or relationship, or love. Our queering here allows us to question our questions, and demands that we approach the scriptures without our often unquestioned assumptions and expectations.

Our doing so will not necessarily be comfortable. Those who hold power are endlessly unwilling to let go of it. In the church, this often takes the form of calling 'heresy' by self-proclaimed defenders of 'orthodoxy'. Such terms have been so abused and misused (and weaponised) over the centuries, and in particular the last half century, as to have lost much of the value that they previously had. We might simply think of heresy as being something which says less about God rather than more – it is quite simply not reasonable to apply this to queer attempts to interpret scripture. We say less about God when there are fewer people in the room asking the questions, and when the questions from the margins are dismissed out of hand as 'unorthodox'.

These same heresy-hunters will approach passages such as Ephesians 5 and interpret it as unchanging and singular, refusing to acknowledge the cultural context or the fact that the underlying theological motifs and concepts explored in such a passage might not be inescapably intertwined with the author's working out of these in pastoral practice. This passage reads in an increasingly disturbing and unhappy way to the contemporary ear. The NRSV's subheading 'The Christian Household' appears little more than an absurdity – and an offensive one at that. Few heterosexual Christian households behave in this way, yet this passage is often used – because of the marriage metaphor – to argue for the necessity of male and female in marriage.

This is interesting from a number of perspectives. The first

– and the most sinister – is the continued belief, albeit one hidden beneath the surface, in a number of Christian circles that there is indeed a hierarchical relationship between men and women. Men are leaders – they are strong, hunter-gatherers, who offer protection and security to the family. Women are home-makers – they are gentle, and kind, and loving, offering stability and nurture. Within the church, this kind of misogyny (and basic anthropological mistake) is dressed up in the language of 'complementarianism' – a theological belief that springs from and ultimately perpetuates the normativity the church is enslaved to.

Yet there remains a more subtle interpretation of this passage, which is willing to go one step towards recognising that the power dynamics included here might be culturally conditioned, or that the author is making subtle comments about husbands showing *love* which themselves might be countercultural, yet which does all of this whilst ensuring the reinforcement of the cis-heterosexual narrative. Such interpretations might allow churches with women's ordination, and healthier relationships 'between the sexes', moving even towards a recognition that radical equality is of God, and yet the interpretative method used is applied inconsistently. LGBTQI people remain beyond the realms of the imagination employed – there remains a belief that they cannot possibly be amongst those to whom this passage is speaking. Thus, passages which on the face of it appear to say more about cis-heterosexual (in)equality and patriarchy end up being used to oppose LGBTQI flourishing. Herein we find the power of pervasive cis-heteronormativity.

RADICAL EQUALITY AS THEOLOGICAL MOTIF

Let us return for a moment to the idea of radical equality. As has become clear, it is not going to be possible for those who ideologically oppose LGBTQI love to recognise what scripture might have to say about same-sex or same-gender relationships. Such a recognition would require a better primary question – asking what scripture has to say about relationship *per se* rather than about a particular type of twenty-first century relationships. We will return to a fuller discussion of marriage in a few chapters' time – for now, it is enough to state the obvious, which is that one's sexuality or gender identity is not a relevant category when asking whether an individual can form a covenantal relationship with another person. Indeed, even this is perhaps to place the emphasis too much on the concept of relationships rather than relationship. We might be better to state clearly that one's sexuality or gender identity are entirely irrelevant to the quality of relationship that any individual might form with another.

We will cover sex more fully in the next chapter, but one of the frequent challenges to this simple statement of fact is that only some people are *rightly* called to sexual relationship, seen to be a discrete form of relationship. This challenge is normally presented whereby one group (the heterosexual) is called to sexual relationship, whereas all others are not. As we have seen and shall see, this is defective reasoning, and it suggests that there is a qualitative difference in the nature of relationality cis-heterosexuals and others should – and hence can, as our religious laws speak not about what we ought to do but what we in actuality can do – form.

It is our contention here that even the process of attempting to separate out 'the sexual act' as a detached and discrete thing in itself is a logical wrong turn. The sexual is not so easily isolated from wider human experience and existence – indeed, we must be very careful to ensure that our definitions and distinctions are actually useful ways of engaging with these questions (both biologically/psychologically and theologically). That is not to say that we cannot have important discussions about intimacy, fidelity, and the overt sexual act, but we must be alert to our oversimplification and unconscious association of 'the sexual' with 'the reproductive'.

This is to say that the idea that particular people are not called to be sexual beings *per se* is plainly absurd. It is not only absurd – it is impossible, and ignores the reality of the human person. That is not to say that all can, do, and should express themselves in genital acts (again, an unfortunate phrase), but it is also to make clear that those acts are part and parcel of a wider sexual self that is not solely associated with reproduction. It is notable that 'biology' is co-opted when it suits the cis-heteronormative narrative, but not when it isn't!

Thus, we know that there is nothing ontologically different about queer people – created in the same Image of God, endowed with the same human qualities which include the yearning for and openness to relationship in all its fulness, reflecting the nature of God and thus the nature of reality. When we observe queer experience, we find people who are open to covenant in a way that is in no material way different to anyone else. The scriptural talk of covenant and relationality speak to queer people in the same way as anyone else. 'There is no longer Jew or Greek; there is no longer slave or free; there is no longer male and female, for all of you are one in Christ Jesus' (Galatians 3:28) – such words have a meaning if we are willing to hear them without first baptising them with culture.

FROM RELATIONSHIPS TO RELATIONSHIP

In our thinking so far, we have found ourselves time and time again tempted to focus on relationships rather than relationship, and it is worth once again bringing the focus back to the centrality of relationship, rather than relationships, in the Biblical narrative. The institutional church's endless focus on the latter has meant that our approach to the scriptures has been skewed in a way that has been unhelpful to queer and non-queer – unhelpful in different ways and to different degrees, perhaps, but ultimately unhelpful to the mission and ministry of the church of God.

For example, our contemporary cultural – and ecclesial – deification of the nuclear family as the ultimate goal and end of human society has done grave damage to the church and our ability to speak counterculturally. A religion built on the action of the God who enters quite unexpectedly into social convention and shakes it to its core has co-opted the holy family to become an unsuspecting and entirely inappropriate sponsor of a cultural idol, an idol of the peripheral expression rather than the theological core. The overvaluing of this particular motif leads us to a Christianity that feels leagues removed from its radical origins, allowing it to become a tool of social propriety and respectability that flies in the face of so much of the Gospel narratives.

Such a deification is, perhaps, most seen in the Roman Catholic Church, yet we see it too in the Church of England and around the Anglican Communion. We will reassess the focus on 'sexual propriety' in our next chapter, but we must be aware, too, of the assimilation of middle-class and petit bourgeois values into the way the church chooses to present itself to the wider world, with endless talk of families and pedestrian social pursuits which aim to present bishops, in particular, as 'safe' and unthreatening – a particularly dull form of cultural Christianity. Queer theology's emphasis on class, wealth and wider socioeconomics is key here – and the dynamics of social propriety are ultimately inseparable from patriarchy and cis-heteronormativity. The church's unwillingness to challenge this, and indeed its seeming desire to strengthen, export, and perpetuate it, speaks volumes about the cultural influences unconsciously playing a role in the life of the contemporary church.

For example, queer families – beyond the conventional sense of children living with adults towards a wider idea of groups of people brought into intimacy through chosen-ness and friendship, as many queer groupings are – offer a different and complementary vision of relationship to that of exclusive (or otherwise) intimate relationships, one that embodies themes such as solidarity, companionship, shared experience and commitment to shared growth. This deeply theological expression of relationship, perhaps best described as 'virtuous friendship', is a relative newcomer to cultural understandings of marriage, which the queer writer Mandy Ford describes as 'the mutual gaze on God' that couples (and we might argue chosen communities of friendship) are now encouraged to exemplify.[3] Virtuous friendship surely has much to recommend it – not least in the development of church communities – and the shared experience and yet diverse experiences of queer people, most particularly queer people of faith, has much to teach the church about how this might be reflected in our Christian life together.

These queer communities of friendship embody many of the Biblical themes of relationship and love that we have touched on a number of times during this chapter. In such communities, it is not because of a professed ontological difference (the aforementioned complementarity) between 'the sexes' that enables a couple to reflect this theological relationality, but rather the active choice of those within such groups to seek out relationship with one another. This refusal to acknowledge social or 'natural' categories as having theological worth – in other words, this queerness – is reflected in the relationality we see in God's relationship with God's people. God's relationship with God's people is, thus, queer, and we might ask too about the queerness at the heart of the Trinitarian relatedness. There is much more to be said on this – but for now, let us simply recognise the theological possibilities that queer community raises, and the poverty we are led to as a church if we refuse to recognise how it might speak to us.

[3]   Mandy Ford, *God, Gender, Sex and Marriage* (London: Jessica Kingsley, 2019) p.106

CONCLUSION

Giving the theological primacy to relationship over relationships and beginning our theological questioning with relationship rather than relationships, is the first step in embracing a richer and more enlivening engagement with scripture and the theological tradition when it comes to understanding human flourishing. Our recognition, and acceptance, that the scriptures do indeed have much to say to queer people, on the same terms as those who are not queer, means that we can move to a theological anthropology beyond reproduction and gender complementarity.

Theologies that deny queer people access to the Bible's message of relationship, or which suggest that an intrinsic disorder leads to our being excluded from fully living this message, fly in the face of all that we are called to hear and know about God, God's relationship with the created order, and God in Godself. They ultimately degrade us, and deny our humanity, making us less-than and in some ontological way deficient. They deny the Image of God in us and in so doing place an unbridgeable gulf between queer existence and God. To do so is as absurd as it is wrong.

Having pressed a reset on our engagement with scripture in this way, we must now turn to the thorny topic of sex and sexuality. If queer people are called to relationship then we are also called to desire, and intimacy, and self-giving love that – for many – finds its human fulfilment in sexual union. We must now ask not whether one thing or another is permitted, but what queerness has to say about sexuality more generally. It is to that task we now turn.

5

QUEERING ... THE NATURE OF SEX

The time has come to talk about sex. That is, the time has come not only in this book but in the church, too. In my own church, the Church of England, the charge will doubtless be laid that we have been talking about sex for decades, and most particularly in recent years through the *Living in Love and Faith* project. The reality, though, is that the one thing we haven't really talked about at all is sex itself. We've talked about other people having it, and whether they should or shouldn't be doing so. We've talked about reproduction (a rather limited understanding of procreation) and the begetting of children. We've talked euphemistically about intimacy. What we haven't really spent any time at all on is the mechanics of the whole thing – vaginal, anal and oral penetration, non-penetrative sex, masturbation (alone or mutual or otherwise), foreplay. We haven't talked about sex for pleasure or sex for fun. We haven't talked about the joys and the fears of sex, or the icky bits we'd rather not discuss in front of our grandparents. In fact, for all our claims that we have been talking about sex, the one thing we haven't talked about is – sex.

It's absolutely time to break the taboo – not only because sex is important, which it is, but also because it is also not the only important thing about living the Christian life. In recent years we have been told that our approach to same-sex, same-gender relationships is a mark of orthodoxy, which is an absolute bucket of baloney, yet it has become abundantly clear that far too many people are too scared to say anything about it in case they get accused of being on the wrong side of God, or – indeed – of offending 'Him'. In a meeting of the Church of England's College of Bishops, one prelate is reported to have said 'well maybe we could just say nothing about sex at all' in the Pastoral Guidance that the bishops had agreed to release to talk about ... sex. It would be comic if it weren't so tragic – and so serious.

We need to say something about sex because not to do so means the church abrogating our responsibility to the most vulnerable in society, and downplaying the obvious sexual sins that we – as a church – have been complicit in. Our safeguarding processes – and the public perception of them – remain scandalously underdeveloped and untrusted. The plain fact that bishops, priests, and others in positions of authority in the church have raped, sexually assaulted, abused, and leched over those in their care is a matter of public record. It is also a plain fact that many have gotten away with it. For an organisation whose culture and practices not only permitted but appears to have enabled sexual abuse to throw its arms up in defeat and say it has nothing to say might appear at least understandable at first glance, but it is entirely unacceptable. Our faith has much to say about sex. We have just failed to listen, not least because we have been asking the wrong questions.

That listening seems, to me, to be one of the key ways that queer theology can help the church to climb out of the enormous hole it finds itself in. When the church does deign to speak about sex, it manages to do so in a way that best resembles a mix of Victorian and early twentieth century prudism, served on a bed of prejudice and intentional misunderstanding. Our inability to speak to the world about sex is in no small part because we seem unwilling to actually listen to what sex might mean to the average person to whom we intend to speak. We appear to see our conversations about sex being entirely one-way, where the church decides what is and what is not permitted (those unhelpful categories making themselves known once again) and lectures the public about 'God's will' in these matters, without a moment's introspection. It's not that the church has nothing to say about sex – it's that what we have to say is so childish, so facile, so banal, so embarrassing, that nobody, including those inside our church, is remotely interested in hearing it.

One group of people who have had a lot to say about sex – indeed, who have had the courage to do so – has been queer people. The usual prejudice will doubtless show itself here amongst those who wish to decry queer people as solely interested in sex, but it is interesting (putting it mildly) that those in the church who have pushed that line have all-too-frequently themselves been found in rather compromising positions! The reality is that queer people – as people who have been, and in many cases continue to be, pushed out of respectable and 'polite' society – simply have the courage to talk about those things that embarrassment, or social convention, or propriety, or plain old lack of imagination have prevented others from discussing.

QUEER HONESTY

Far from disparaging queer culture's willingness to talk about sex, we should be grateful for it – in the church and in the world more widely. Nor should we imagine that there is one monochrome, singular understanding of sex amongst queer people – just as there is no one, single type of queer person either. Whilst it is easier and requires less effort to paint all queer people in the way that is most likely to cause scandal at any particular moment in time (for example, the unforgivable and yet tolerated behaviour of elected members of the General Synod of the Church of England in their endless pursuit of the outrage card, linking queer people and queer theology with paedophilia), this is no way to go about a serious debate.

It is unfortunate that some of the loudest voices in church debates around matters of sex and sexuality debate in bad faith, deliberately misconstruing ideas and views in order to more easily 'win' an argument, and in recent years such people have been set like dogs on queer Christians, seeking who they may devour. Yet whilst such people make a real debate difficult (and should simply be disengaged from), we must also recognise that some of what queer people are saying out loud really does remain taboo for many in the church. The mere willingness to discuss casual sex, or BDSM, or fetish, remains for some a bridge too far. Yet this is to make the age-old mistake of pretending that if you don't mention something it will go away. It won't. The church needs to be adult enough to have these kinds of conversations in good faith, not least because if she won't then the rest of the world will simply discount her as a conversation partner. That's not to say that the church should say that every sex practice is something of which it approves (admitting the terrible dynamics that this belies), but it is to say that taboo, embarrassment, disgust and propriety are not how a religion should decide how to engage in public conversation.[1]

Allowing ourselves to debate and discuss such an important topic as sex on the playing field of propriety leads us back to a place where either nothing is said, or where normativity – that great cousin of propriety – is allowed to dictate our terms in what should be a serious theological

---

[1] We might think here of the extraordinary outcry by some church authority figures against drag performances, including by those church figures who seek to – scandalously – portray these as paedophilic (e.g., in the pearl-clutching opposition to drag queen story-time). This is part of a wider church narrative that seeks to keep anything that might remind humankind that they are embodied sexual beings away from church in the name of propriety. This trend is an alarming one, because it fails to take into account the facts – that we are, indeed, sexual beings and that **all** of our selves is called into the dance of faith.

enterprise. 'Sex is for marriage' may sound simple, yet it is entirely inadequate in formulating a response to the reality of human sexual experience, queer or otherwise. It is in our failure to even engage with questions of 'why', beyond the rather petulant 'because God and the church says so', that we ultimately abrogate a responsibility that is rightly ours. It is also through this slavish obedience to respectability that we end up simply trying to subsume queer people in marriage rather than do any of the hard work we are called to do. Yes, of course LGBTQI people should be able to get married – so much is self-evident – but if that is our end point, then we have done little more than made queers respectable, and in the process lost all sight of the enriching challenge that queerness might bring to our church.

THE PROBLEM OF SEX

Our duty, as a church, is twofold (at least). Firstly, we need to suspend our prejudice and open our ears to what queer lives and loves might tell us. Secondly, we must ask ourselves a simple yet devastating follow-on: what is distinctively Christian about the sexual ethic that we espouse? Just as importantly, does there need to be a particular 'Christian' sexual ethic? What is sex? What is its nature, what is its purpose, and what is its meaning? Tired old references made to reproduction (what is so often meant by 'procreation', as we shall discuss below) are quite simply not enough. We know that non-queers, even those in totally normative relationships, are having sex that is non-reproductive, and the church doesn't condemn it (you cannot become pregnant through oral sex, for example).

There are, of course, bizarre, casuistical arguments made, particularly by those still wedded to teaching documents such as *humanae vitae*,[2] that suggest that each sexual act has to

---

[2]   A most unfortunate encyclical in the papacy of Pope St Paul VI, which in many ways ran a coach and horses through the potential that this papacy

be 'open to reproductive purposes', which – frankly – are an insult to the intelligence of the proposer and the hearer. The Anglican Communion, in its acceptance of contraception,[3] cannot rely on these kind of arguments – once contraception is permitted, sex is not solely for reproduction. Yet even if we were to give the arguments that sex is for reproduction only some credence (which we shouldn't given the church's own application of these rules – neither a woman who has had a hysterectomy or a man who has had a permanent vasectomy are open to reproductive purposes in any way whatsoever, and yet are perfectly free to have sex), we should also be honest that non-queers are having sex that is not penile-vaginal penetration (and, indeed, some queers *are* having penile-vaginal intercourse that *is* open to reproduction). The church seems to be deafeningly silent about that.

Of course, the argument might be made that such 'non-reproductive sex' (for example, oral sex) builds up the intimacy of the marriage bed, and who can argue with that? Indeed, Resolution 13 of the 1930 Lambeth Conference did just this, stating that 'intercourse between husband and wife as the consummation of marriage has a value of its own within that sacrament, and that thereby married love is enhanced and its character strengthened'.[4] All the evidence that we have suggests that sex within relationships of those of the same

---

might have embodied in the wake of Vatican II The encyclical was an effective ban on 'artificial means' [sic] of contraception – something that at the time was much more of an open conversation in Roman Catholic circles than is often imagined (readers may be interested that the papal document went against the Papal Commission on Birth Control which had been originally

set up by the saintly Pope John XXIII, the patron saint of the author!). The text is available here: https://www.vatican.va/content/paul-vi/en/encyclicals/documents/hf_p-vi_enc_25071968_humanae-vitae.html [accessed October 7th 2023].

[3]   As discussed here by Bishop Richard Harries in 'The Anglican acceptance of contraception', *Transformation* Vol. 13:3 pp.2-4. An argument is made that Pope St Paul VI felt constrained by what was in many ways a Roman Catholic response to this decision by the Lambeth Conference in 1930, *Casti connubii* (issued by Pope Pius XI).

[4]   Ibid

sex or gender does this in precisely the same way. It is hard to see opposition to this kind of sex *only* between people of the same sex or gender, then, as being anything other than bare-faced queerphobia.

A further argument might then be made – indeed, is made – that this is because sex of any kind should be kept within marriage, and because marriage is between a man and a woman, it is not queerphobic but simply in-keeping with this injunction. We will address the meat of this below, but for now the sheer absurdity of such a circular argument needs to be made out loud, not least because of the import given to this in recent discussions within the Church of England. Great howls of outrage were heard in the General Synod of February 2023 when it became apparent that sex outside of marriage might be allowed – howls from the very people who were working night and day to ensure couples of the same sex or gender were excluded from marriage. Whilst this is a clever political game to play, it is logically faulty – we cannot simply say sex is for marriage without explaining *why* that is the case, and we are no longer able to use the reproduction argument to do so. Sex within opposite-sex couples is not necessarily reproductive, and the sex that is not reproductive may not be even indirectly leading to reproductive sex. The chain is broken – the queerphobia remains.

Other arguments to only exclude same-sex and gender couples from experiencing sexual intimacy do exist, but most of these rely on arguments directly related to keeping queers out of marriage rather than on sex itself, and we will engage with these in the next chapter. For now, it is worth reiterating the central point – it is not non-reproductive sex that the institutional church has a problem with, it is non-reproductive sex amongst queers. In other words, and in more graphic terms, it is entirely acceptable for a bishop's husband to engage in anal sex with her, but it is apparently not acceptable for a gay cleric to have anal sex with his partner. This particular example is used, because in a Church of England meeting about sex, when a senior female cleric was asked when she last had anal sex with her husband, she took umbrage and stated that she found the question offensive. What was pointed out to her was that this was precisely the kind of inappropriate, intrusive, prurient questioning that queer clergy were expected to countenance – indeed that the church had itself sanctioned. It appeared that the het-privilege and cis-heteropatriarchy – and the queerphobia implicit in it – came a shock.

THE NATURE OF SEX

Before we go much further, we must refocus on a question that we met earlier in this chapter – what, exactly, are we talking about? What is sex? The institutional church seems to like banning it – particularly when it comes to queers – but what exactly is it that we are talking about?[5] How might we define it? In other words, when is it that queers start to do something which they shouldn't do? Is it a discrete thing? How might it be separated out? How might queers know that they've gone a step too far? Why is it quite so dangerous?

The simplest way of answering this question would be to make reference to penises and vaginas, but we can't do that without immediately falling into the trap of queerphobia and circular argument. Indeed, in a sense, because the large majority of queer sex does not risk (for want of a better term) reproduction, then the 'risk' from it is lower in that regard. So our next question might be – is this all about penetration? A brief foray through the 'Christian' anti-queer literature might make you believe just that, and in particular might make you wonder whether women having sex had crossed the minds of many of those seeking to clamp down on queerness. Yet whilst penetration as a particular form of sexual intimacy is

---

[5] These questions were covered in some detail in Chapter 4 of *Queer Holiness*, but deserve attention here, given the ongoing refusal of the church to engage with this key area.

clearly of importance when discussing sex, it is by no means the only thing we ought to be thinking of. Queer people might be more willing to talk about it, but the idea of a grey area in sexual behaviour is not alien to non-queers either. The recognition that we are sexual beings, and that the sexual involves more than merely the penetrative (or, indeed, merely the consciously aroused physical) is widespread in the scientific literature – and, with even moderate levels of introspection, in the human experience too. That this is the case suggests that we must do some more thinking about ideas such as continence, fidelity, exclusivity – indeed, we must ask whether and why such terms are relevant at all.

Such questions are complicated and uncomfortable but essential. It is no small wonder that religion has in the main attempted to keep sex boxed in as a set of actions, which can then be categorised and sorted into the 'yes' and the 'no' of valid behaviour. Once we open this up, then we need to develop a much more thoughtful and complex conversation about what rightly ordered sexuality looks like. In even the most continent of individuals, the sexual urge cannot and will not be entirely abrogated – but more complicated still, even were it to be so, the underlying dynamics of human interaction retain sexual elements. This is, surely, true in those who choose not to express themselves in sexual activity (for example those who are celibate) and those who are asexual. That is not to say that 'everything is sex', but it is to say that the neat, fine dividing lines between the sexual and the sensual become increasingly difficult to define, that 'sexual activity' itself becomes culturally defined to some degree, and that the 'sexual' forms a constituent part of our being social.

To put that another way, our sexuality is part of our relationship-forming nature, and because of that, our sexuality is an intensely theological thread in our ontology and identity as human beings made in the Image of God. It is for this reason that the church must have something to say about sex, or rather must have something to say about the role of the erotic and the sexual in our relating to one another, yet also a reason that the church needs to engage in such conversations by first recognising and understanding the real rather than the pretend. Queering here once again draws our attention to the unreality at the heart of so much of what the church has to say about sex, and draws our attention back to the reality in plain sight. It is through a denial of queerness that we are driven to a denial of social sexuality – and if we deny that, then we are driven towards our contemporary pedestrian sexual ethics. We do a disservice to the church corporate in so doing.

Even at the level of the sexual act, queerness reminds us of the absurdity of our current position. Bisexual and pansexual people are surely a significant challenge to the church's current thinking on 'what goes where, when and how'. Viewed through the cis-heteronormative lens, such people's lives can be split up into the licit and the illicit – their engaging in sex acts with someone of the opposite sex is permissible, whilst their engaging in sex acts with someone of the same sex is not permissible. It is for this reason that even institutional church teaching appeared to recommend forms of 'conversion therapy' – failing to recognise that sexual attraction (and, dare we say, love) cannot be switched off at will. Yet viewing sexual behaviour in this way is to completely ignore the reality of the human condition, and viewed without the normative lens is seen to be patently absurd. This lens distorts reality by suggesting that such acts are categorizable, denying huge swathes of the underlying social-sexual dynamics in an individual, and – worse – making moral judgements based on such faulty logic.

Once we appreciate that bisexual or pansexual people's sexuality needs to be approached from a wider perspective rather than merely from focus on the genitals of the person towards whom it is directed, then our ability to categorise in this way surely fails. *Contra* 'hate the sin, love the sinner', the sexual drive is not neatly separable from the sexual act, and nor is the sexual drive neatly separable from the psychological, the social, the neurological, ultimately the anthropological. There is nothing substantially different in the sex drive towards different sexes or genders in bisexual or pansexual people. We retain the option, of course, of admitting that our (that is, the church's) problem with queer people is actually that we believe them to be intrinsically disordered, yet many would be unwilling to take that step. The issue is we need to engage with precisely these questions if we are to engage with human beings as human beings and not as a different wished-for species. Removing the blinkers of normativity and making real human experience our starting point means we need to rethink the whole enterprise.

Questions such as this highlight some of the themes of the last chapter once again. For example, whilst as Christians we surely accept that our bodies have metaphysical value, does our sex and our gender? If so, what is this value and from where do we derive our reasoning (more of that in our chapter on marriage)? This raises age-old questions such as 'will our bodies be sexed in heaven'? Will everyone in heaven be straight? That is, will we have been 'cured' of our transgressive sexuality?

Intelligent attempts at answers to such questions might suggest that human outward 'worldly' expressions of sexuality are unlikely to be found in heaven, given sexuality's playing a part in human desire which – at the culmination of all things – will be rightly directed towards God. Yet this does not make the questions go away. Arguments from The Fall and others which suggest non-cis-heteronormative sexual desire is wrongly ordered and directed would necessitate us accepting that it is somehow in need of more redemption than cis-heteronormative sexual desire – in other words, cis-heteronormative sexual desire needs purification and realignment, but queer sexual desire needs total refitting! This does suggest that whilst cis-heterosexual desire is in some coherent way part of the economy of heaven, queer sexual desire is explicitly excluded, and so some form of 'cure' is needed.

QUEERING ... THE NATURE OF SEX

SEX AND GENDER AS METAPHYSICAL CATEGORIES

To return to the metaphysical importance – or otherwise – of sex and gender, we might best separate this into three questions. Firstly, does sex and gender have metaphysical import for the individual Christian in their life in this world? Secondly, does sex and gender have metaphysical import for their relationships with and relating to others? Thirdly, does sex and gender have any eternal ramifications?

We have begun this exploration in our discussion of heavenly desire. Yet there is surely more to ask here about the created order and the place of sex and gender within it. At one end, we might look towards 'nature' for our answer. Surveying the created order, it is clear that sexual reproduction is not the only show in town – and that our XY dimorphism (with all the caveats that are usually so carelessly ignored by theologians) is not itself the only form of dimorphism. We might from this simply state that sexual dimorphism (laying gender aside for one moment) is merely a means to an end – a way for the human species to reproduce with the introduction of variation for the benefit of evolutionary processes. At the other end, we might take a prescriptive (rather than descriptive) approach to Genesis 1:27, 'male and female he created them', and – like many conservative theologians – suggest that sexual dimorphism is purposive beyond reproduction. In this view, human anatomy is inseparable from human existence – it is infused with godly design and cannot be laid aside.

Neither of these approaches is entirely satisfactory. We know that sex does have an impact – beyond the societal – on an individual's experience of the world (albeit that is not the same as suggesting all female experience, for example, is the same), and we also know that dimorphism, whilst the most frequent form of sexual expression, is not the only form. Similarly, we know that such a thing as gender exists, and exists separate from the category of sex (this is not to say that discrete gender categories necessarily exist, but rather that the experience of gender as beyond the category of sex does exist). It is known that cultural and societal forces impact upon the relationship between sex and gender, and that experiences of sex itself can be in tension between anatomy and psychological makeup. Indeed, human beings are not simply the anatomical, and it is extraordinary how, when pontificating on issues of sex and gender, conservative Christians so often privilege the anatomical over the psychological, with the implication that the former is real and that the latter is not (and, indeed, there is very little reflection on the relationship of either of these to the soul – and the danger of patriarchy's colonisation of the soul). Hence trans* Christians are told that their anatomy is 'right' and their psychology is 'wrong' – without recognising that their psychology is itself just as 'biological' as their anatomy!

In any conversations around sex and gender, we cannot simply ignore the reproductive aspects of sexual dimorphism, but similarly we must not fall into the trap of suggesting that this is the only role of (generally dimorphic) sexual characteristics in human life. Similarly, the existence of gender and its interaction with sex suggests that from an experiential perspective, these two things do – through their impact on self-understanding, identity (and identity formation), and experience of the world –have theological import not only for the individual but also for our relating to one another. Yet that is far from saying that this theological import is about categorisation or prescription. In other words, we can recognise that sex and gender exist and impact on one's life (and hence one's relationship with God and others) without imbuing them with sacred immutability and suggesting that they are the prime director of human behaviour.

We might thus argue that sex and gender's theological importance comes from how they impact upon us, rather than because of their pre-existing us as theological categories. Much ultimately hangs on the interpretation of Biblical passages that make reference to sex (and gender), such as the Genesis passage above, to which reference is made in the Gospels. Given that we know that male and female are not the only forms of sexual expression, our favouring of a descriptive rather than a prescriptive reading of this Genesis passage seems justified – that is, 'God created *both* male and female (and everything in between)' rather than 'God *only* created male and female'. That God created the entirety of the human race in God's own image seems to be a rather broader theological vision than the alternative interpretation, and it is somewhat far-fetched to imagine that the writers of Genesis were using their creation narrative to enforce sex and gender binaries as we are often led to believe. Given that we do not know the chromosomal makeup of a single Biblical character (most especially, perhaps, Our Lord Himself!), it is surely a bizarre twisting of scripture to suggest that Genesis is all about chromosomes.

There is much more to be said about identity, experience, the unhelpful nature of categorisation, and the even more unhelpful desire to read such categories into scripture when it is read through the normative lens. For now, let us return to the final of the questions highlighted above – does sex and gender have eternal ramifications or are they of eternal importance (however we might experience that in ourselves and others)? We might further split this question into – does sex and gender continue beyond this world, and do sex and gender *as categories* rather than simply as experienced realities have theological import – that is, do they precede us and define us?

Of course, these latter two questions are linked, and a full answer would require a wider discussion of the role of time in the context of eternity! We might ask, however, whether God created us to experience life in a sexed manner – and our answer may indeed be a highly qualified yes, given that this is how we experience life, although a 'yes' which rejects a simplistic drive towards binary categorisation. We might then ask the same question of gender – and whilst we might recognise that gender is part of human experience, we might be more reticent to suggest there is anything objective whatsoever about gender (for example, we already know that gender roles are fluid between cultures). Our key question on sex, therefore, is about its purposive nature beyond its reproductive potential – where we might see sexual dimorphism to be necessary, but primarily to serve a function (although a function which itself may have metaphysical import, and a function from which particular experiences are certainly derived, for example in the case of childbearing, which themselves may have metaphysical value). Our question, then, really comes down to whether 'categorised sex' is real – not whether it is the norm expressed in this-world human existence, but whether it is theologically real. Does the binarism of sexual categories really matter – do they really exist, or is their use a worldly one of convenience?

As we have seen above, it is certainly true that in most cases most sexual characteristics do cluster together (for example, ovary, uterus, vagina, clitoris, breasts and less body hair) and these clusters are helpful to some degree in discussions of the human person as experienced by both self and other. Our key question, however, as theologians and Christians, is whether this clustering actually *matters* in and of itself. More specifically, is strict sexual dimorphism essential to our understanding of the Gospel? Is our (cultural) association of particular sexes and particular genders – again, something that is found in the experience of many but not all people – essential to our understanding of the Gospel? We know, for example, that there is no one experience of being a woman or a man, but do we need nonetheless to make use of these categories if we are to talk about God? Are these categories, however flawed, still necessary in the theological enterprise – indeed are they fundamental in God's way of defining us as human beings?

It is on this that much of the debate on rightly ordered sexuality rests, and in particular on the role of the male, the man. There is much debate in conservative Christian circles about the place and reality of trans* people, but more often than not this is really reduced to receptive male penetrative anal sex – the trans* people who are in the firing line are very frequently those born with external male sexual characteristics who experience dysphoria in these sexed bodies. Their breaking of the sex dimorphic boundary is regarded as a particularly egregious sin in the same way that male same-sex, same-gender couples appear more detestable than female-female (an interesting window into the directionality of patriarchal attitudes). 'Men', here, are seen offering their bodies to 'other men' in a degrading way – their masculinity is being compromised and indeed willingly surrendered. This appears to be the final taboo in conservative theology.

Given all we know about queer experience, about the different ways that sex is experienced in normal human variation, about the complex interrelationship between sex and gender expression, about the variation beyond sexual dimorphism, and given our recognition that sexed bodies have implications beyond reproductive potential (for example, in sexual attraction, itself part of our social selves), our answer to our question above perhaps finds itself in the grey area between yes and no. Yes, we might argue, sex matters – or, perhaps, *sex as a continuum* matters, given the way that sex and gender cannot be simply categorised. In other words, our sexual (and gender) *characteristics* matter, and are so intricately and intimately associated with the human experience as to form part of the definition of being human, but to reduce this to an untrue, one-size-fits-all binary, in which diversity of experience is sacrificed on the altar of normativity, is quite wrong.

This, then, helps us address the questions of eternity and pre-existing sex and gender categorisation. It is of the essence of queering that neat categories are unhelpful in our understanding of the world because they obscure the truth, and here we see why that is the case. It is certainly true that the sex continuum (that is, chromosomal, gonadal, somatic) plays a part in our development and self-understanding, our expression and experience, as human persons, but it is one contributor amongst many and does not hold the primacy for human life. Indeed, being willing to recognise the contribution of the sex continuum whilst not being in thrall to it as all-encompassing categories allows us to respect the diversity of human life more fully as it is lived. This is not a denial of sexual characteristics, of genetics, or of anatomy – yet nor is it a denial of the integrated human person to which these elements contribute but do not define.[6]

Once we appreciate this, then we also begin to recognise how much of our recourse to 'Biblical' material on matters of sex and gender are little more than reading out the implications of the lenses we have already put on before approaching scripture. When we are freed from the need to find sex and gender as categorical rather than continual – and no less valid because of this – then we are able to more readily approach the scriptures with St Paul's 'no longer male and female' as our guiding light. Indeed, we are more able to approach God without the encumbrance of binarism and in doing so, even find ways to talk about God that don't necessitate our gendering and sexing Him or Her before talking about God. Once the essential sex binary is no longer the guiding light, then we can more readily listen to the voices of experience and recognise them as part and parcel of the continuum of God-given human diversity. In many ways, this strengthens our ability to listen and to properly hear the experience of gender-based violence, of the persistent impact of patriarchy, of the reality of our having sexual bodies. It also strengthens our ability to see the real and not the pretend – however *practically* useful we might

---

[6] Of course, we might ask questions as to whether sexual intercourse will continue beyond death. From our arguments in this book, we might suggest that the answer is both yes and no, depending on what we are referring to! The sexual is so integral to the embodied reality of human life that it surely has some part to play in the life of the Resurrection (as part of our integrated, redeemed selves), but that is not the same as suggesting that the embodied life of the Resurrection will require our being 'sexual' in the way we are on Earth. There is much to ponder here!

find pretending that binarism exists to be. As theologians we are not called to speak in the language of the practically useful – we are called to speak about reality.

We have wandered somewhat from the thorny issue of sex – in its other meaning. It is time, now, to return to it – its purpose and meaning – and ask whether, given what we have said so far, we might have more to learn about human sexuality.

6

QUEERING ... THE MEANING OF SEX

In our last chapter, we touched on the nature of sex – in both meanings of the word. Concepts and understandings of both meanings of sex, together with gender, are absolutely key to our being able to start asking questions about rightly ordered sexuality. In this chapter, we will engage first with the purpose and meaning of sex, two closely interwoven questions which require answers not only for queer people but for others, too, despite the burden normally being placed on our shoulders. As we have said, in the Church of England's current understanding, sex is not only about reproduction, despite that being an occasional refrain in these debates – and if it were, then we would surely be attempting to police non-queers in the same way that we police queer lives. So, we might ask ourselves, what is it for – and what is it not for? And why should we care?

SEX AS INTERCOURSE

One of the niceties of the English language is the use of the word 'intercourse' to neatly separate out sex as being (that is, the categories we addressed in the last few pages) and sex as doing. Intercourse – communication – is, perhaps the very simplest answer to the question that we have just posed, and in many ways we could leave the discussion there. Sex, whether it be casual or committed, queer or not, penetrative or not, is always a form of communication – and yet that communication is by no means uniform. Sex without consent is a radically different form of communication to sex with consent; sex between a long-standing monogamous couple is a very different form of communication to sex on a one-night stand between university students, or sex for pay. Thus, whilst sex is most certainly communication, the nature of that communication and its impact on those involved (including, in the context of unfaithfulness, on the wronged party) cannot and must not be over-simplified or discussed in one-dimensional ways. Sex matters because our embodied existence matters, and an invasion of this most personal of human spaces is rightly condemned by the secular and the religious almost without exception.

In our last chapter, we touched on the very challenging nature of categorising actions as sexual or as non-sexual. Having now seen the futility of a reliance on categories of sex in its other meaning, let us return to this challenge. One of the key implications of refusing sexual categorisation is the complexity that is lent to any conversation that seeks to categorise acts as sexual or otherwise, and hence licit or illicit between two individuals. Meeting individuals first as individuals rather than first as categories means that questions such as 'may this person with a penis penetrate this person with a penis' become increasingly obsolete in questions of sexual intercourse. Instead, our questions need to be deeper and more engaged with the nature of that intercourse – indeed, we might ask ourselves to what degree this intercourse really matters – and hence to what degree sex matters.

This, of course, flies in the face of the strand of theology that is commonly described as complementarian – theology that requires sexual dimorphism as its cornerstone, on which everything else depends. This theological outlook is clearly inadequate – it fails to speak about the world as it actually is, and it does so by imposing a prior anthropological lens of categorical difference on the scriptures,[1] a lens that is used by its proponents to derive readings of the text that then reinforce the lens. Yet it is worth mentioning here because without such a complementarian outlook – where, crudely, penis fits inside vagina, woman is made for man, categorical sex is theologically real – the arguments against sexual intercourse outside a 'male-female' couple bear very little weight. We mention complementarianism, therefore, to reject it as fundamentally unreal and therefore as fundamentally untheological, and thus to draw attention to the importance of the church moving beyond such limiting understandings of sex and gender. We reject it in order to start having the serious conversation about the meaning of sex that can move beyond 'heterosexual marriage' (on which more in the next chapter) and anatomical fit.

We will address matters of marriage in our next chapter. For some readers, this may be the wrong way around – indeed, for the bishops of the Church of England it appears too much to imagine sex as occurring outside of a 'covenanted relationship' (which, of course, in the case of same-sex, same-gender couples, they cannot bring themselves to call marriage, which is its very definition, as we shall see). Yet here let us move beyond questions of whether or not a covenant exists (or, indeed, whether or not a legal partnership exists, on which more below) and instead focus on the characteristics of intercourse that we might call holy, and *from those characteristics*, build up our understanding of sexual intercourse within covenant. Along the way, we might think, too, about sex outside of covenant – and in so doing, recognise the utter inadequacy of the church's current attitudes to such 'casual sex'.

Our first stopping point on the discussion of sexual intercourse is to recollect the impossibility of entirely separating the sexual self from the wider self. That is not

---

[1]   That is not to suggest that such a lens is well or fully developed, or even conscious. Not all 'anthropologies' are equally valid.

to say that people have not tried to do so, and it is not to suggest that the way the sexual is outwardly and inwardly experienced, portrayed and expressed, is the same between individuals – here is that variety again, and the importance of approaching sexuality with the same level of complex analysis as other anthropological concerns. For some people, there is an intense desire to separate the sexual from the wider self, but such a process is likely to cause significant psychological damage to such individuals.[2]

Casual sex is a good example of a place where the impact of the sexual on the social self, and vice versa, is highly contested. There is not the space and this is not the place to cover the psychological literature that relates to casual sex and its impact, and a brief review of it might suggest not only that the impact of casual sex is likely to be multifactorial and individual dependent, but also that studies on this are anything but conclusive, and often depend on the angle being pursued. What cannot be said is anything categorical – that casual sex is psychologically good or bad for all people. Of course, psychology doesn't give us all the answers but it does provide an important contribution to our development of a theological anthropology that takes real human life seriously. In other words, we cannot simply reject evidence of wellbeing (or otherwise) out of hand – we must have strong grounds to do so. This is unfortunately something that the church does not recognise – suspicion reigns supreme in discussions of the sciences. Yet once we recognise that sexual intercourse is part of the wider human personhood that we are called to, we simply cannot choose to ignore the evidence we don't like whilst accepting the evidence that we do.[3]

---

[2] Of note, this is not the same – necessarily – as a genuinely free choice of celibacy. The psychological defence mechanisms – healthy or otherwise – were covered at length in *Queer Holiness*.

[3] Unfortunately this is another example of the arrogance of much contemporary theology and those who practise it. There is relevant literature to be consulted on these questions, but too many theologians appear to be willing to throw it out before engaging with it. This is little more than crass anti-intellectualism – which never ends well.

SINFUL *AND* BAD?

Of course, that brings into sharp relief the fact that two related but distinct questions need to be asked when we approach matters of human life – in simple terms, firstly is something bad for you, and secondly is something sinful? These two will not always align, not least because the concept of sin takes into account not only whether something will be bad 'for you', but widens this to include both God and fellow humankind (and, perhaps we should add, the entire created order). We are not seeking here to make those questions one and the same. However, what we are seeking to do is ensure that the first question forms part of the interrogation of the second – if something is sinful, why is it sinful? On what grounds?

Arguments for the sinfulness of queer sex comes for those three reasons. Firstly, we have already met examples of how cis-heteronormativity has been baptised by patriarchy and used as hermeneutical tool on Biblical writing, and it is usually from here – or from unchallenged Tradition – that arguments for sinfulness along the lines of 'because God (or the church) says so' come from. They are often dressed up in talk about 'God's design for human life'[4], which neatly ignore the experience or study of actual human lives – such talk is little more than warmed up cis-heteronormative ideology and can be roundly rejected. We hear, too, of somewhat bizarre appeals to the hurt to others (heterosexual marriages being destroyed by same-sex, same-gender couples getting married), and the hurt to the person themselves from not following God's clearly laid plan for their life (a plan which usually means repression of self and various versions of lukewarm 'conversion' therapy). We even hear lurid rubbish about being wrong for the

---

[4] A particularly egregious example was *The Beautiful Story*, a pernicious propaganda film released by the Church of England Evangelical Council in an attempt to sink the *Living in Love and Faith Project* before it had even started.

individual themselves on spurious sexual health grounds.[5]

Yet how little we hear of proper scientific studies being appropriately referenced. We might ask why – and the answer is obvious: because they do not support the cis-heteronormative ideology's proposition. The reality is that being queer – and having sex as queer people – does not lead to poor outcomes. It's the stigma, discrimination and hatred that does[6] – stigma, discrimination and hatred that is all too often sponsored by the religious ideologues who try to lay the blame at the door of the queers. If we are talking about sin, there are worse places to start looking. Yet we queers are told to rejoice at having such people – who continue to peddle this stigma, discrimination and hatred – in our churches, in the name of 'diversity'. Godly diversity should not come at this kind of price.

To return, then, to the purposes of sex, one must – surely, recognising us as integrated human beings – be to build us up as human creatures, both in the way we walk along the world's path but also in the sense of sanctification, our growth in holiness. The church has for too long seen sex as dirty, embarrassing, and something to be avoided, and has much to learn from the secular idea of 'sex positivity'. Sex certainly contains much risk – from the risk of unwieldly desires, to matters of consent, to unplanned pregnancies, to the potential production and perpetration of unhealthy negative impulses within us. Yet sex contains these risks (and more) because it is part of a continuum of human existence that, when rightly directed, can build us up and help us develop more into the people we are called to be.

---

[5] Robert Gagnon being the example *par excellence* of this in the atrocious Chapter 5 of his *The Bible and Homosexual Practice: Texts and Hermeneutics* (Nashville, TN: Abingdon, 2010). If nothing else, this chapter is a salutary lesson in the importance of understanding the scientific method, systematic review, and meta-analysis, if a theologian decides to write about science.

[6] The evidence of this is widespread – a good example might be the Centre for Disease Control and Prevention's page on this topic, accessible here: https://www.cdc.gov/msmhealth/stigma-and-discrimination.htm [accessed October 7th 2023]

We are sexual animals and should rejoice in the pleasure and joy it can bring – rejoicing in this does not mean we make a pretence that there is no risk of the opposite occurring. Being willing to speak openly and honestly about the joys – and fears – of sex in a theological sense is both a sure-fire way to avoid its becoming taboo, with all the attendant horrors that accompany such sexual shame – and also a sure fire way to ensure you are never preferred in the church! Given that bishops are so frequently chosen *because* they have not made public statements on sex beyond the inexcusably banal, it is no small wonder that when they have to lead projects such as *Living in Love and Faith*, they are absolutely unprepared to do so!

We should also be much more vocal – as a theological imperative – about the vulnerability that being sexual beings can create, and most particularly can create in those who face the full brunt of patriarchy. In our churches, this deeply damaging process is a daily lived reality for far too many people – women and non-binary people routinely face misogynistic abuse, and it is a poorly kept secret that large numbers of young men (of varying sexualities) face utterly inappropriate sexual advances and behaviour from older gay men who themselves have failed to move beyond the confines of patriarchy, and simply express it in new ways. Our continued willingness to categorise the sexual and the non-sexual is part and parcel of our inability to recognise let alone appropriately tackle this kind of patriarchal structural violence – we are able to excuse (primarily male) behaviours as being 'not overtly sexual', whilst failing to recognise the complex interplay of reception and intention that characterises the sexual in the human person. Unless something is penetration or kissing, we appear to close our eyes to the sexual potential – and by doing so, we fail to create safe and generative spaces in which all can flourish.

THE CHURCH'S NEED FOR CATEGORISATION

Our problems as a church when it comes to sex are so often tied up in this desperation to categorise. In the Church of England's recent discussions on whether or not clergy may have sex with their partners, the tenor and indeed content of conversations frequently turned to talk of discipline rather than holiness. Our methodology remains one of 'you may, you may not' rather than taking a birds-eye view – a queers-eye view, perhaps – of what being sexual beings is all about in the first place. By such a narrow focus on permissibility, we fail to recognise the role of context and meaning, of the integrated nature of human existence, and of the fluidity of identity and its expression. Before we turn to context and meaning, let us briefly consider this latter point.

Issues in Human Sexuality, the teaching document of the House of Bishops from 1991 which continues to hold much sway in the Church of England (and until recently was used as tool of discipline for queer clergy), made use of the term 'homophile' to describe gay men – a term which, understandably, never really caught on. Yet this points to the fact that the need for categorisation is never far away from church conversations on these topics. The existence of cis-heteronormativity necessitates such categorisation of those who do not fit the box – and thus the more common use of the word 'homosexual' or 'bisexual' to describe non-cis-heterosexuals. The recent rejection of this kind of categorisation and the adoption of the word queer, rather than discrete categories, has caused significant discomfort to those in the conservative wing of the church, not least because of its being a challenge to this categorisation. It is little surprise that such a strong reaction against its use has been seen, as we saw in Part 1.

Once again, and similar to our conversations about sex and gender in the previous chapter, we are not arguing that there is not a norm – there is, because a norm by its nature is descriptive and not prescriptive. There are large numbers of people who would identify as 'gay', or 'lesbian', or 'bisexual', or as a whole host of other different categories of sexuality or gender identity. However, that does not mean that these categories are *real* – it simply means that they are a useful descriptor, or short-hand. For example, using the word queer does not mean that someone is not gay – it simply means that they do not find the more simplistic categorisation as descriptive of their identity as very useful. Different people will have different affinities to different categories or descriptors – but one of the key tenets of queer theology is that that is how those categories remain, merely descriptive.

Here, we return to our opposition to the way that cis-heteronormative ideology has been used to pretend that those categories are real. It is from such a reading that we might approach questions of rightly ordered sexuality from the perspective of 'the homosexual' as opposed to 'the human person'. Such a perspective is unhelpful by its nature (cis-heteronormativity being unreal means that we are already on unsafe ground), but can also be shown to be so through the way it is worked out in practice. Two brief examples – one rather more flippant than the other – may help to illustrate this.

One argument that is frequently made about the 'naturalness' (an unhelpful term) of 'homosexuality' in human beings is reference to examples within 'the natural world'. A classic example would be 'homosexual' penguins – penguins who are seen to have sex with other penguins of the same sexual category. Whilst on face value, this might seem helpful, we need to ask ourselves whether what we are seeing in these penguins is truly 'homosexuality'. To what extent is what we are seeing a categorizable identity, and to what extent is it simply *what we are seeing* – that is, sex between penguins of the same sexual category. There may be some nuances around the socialisation of penguins and the role of sex in this socialisation, but we should surely come down heavily on the second of these options – that what we are seeing is penguins having sex, not 'homosexual' penguins. That may, indeed, have something to teach us about the occurrence of same-sex genital acts in different species – but it is by no means clear that it tells us anything whatsoever about homosexuality (or human sexual expression at all).

Our second example suggests that there may not, indeed, be anything called 'homosexuality' except in relation to 'heterosexuality' (and, we might argue, neither actually exists as a *real* category). Across the world, different cultures have different understandings of same-sex, same-gender sexual intercourse, and – particularly in intra-church dialogue – it may become increasingly difficult to talk to one another because of these different understandings.[7] The use of the identity of 'homosexual' in these conversations actually acts as a conversation stopper rather than starter, leading to a 'dialogue of the deaf' (as David Bagnall reports the former Archbishop of Canterbury, Rowan Williams, as describing it). It may be that churches will still disagree about the illicitness (or otherwise) of same-sex, same-gender sexual intercourse, but our starting point needs to be a recognition that our (frequently White, western) categories are themselves *unreal*. Our discussions would be far more fruitful if we might talk about human beings first, and seek to make use of categories only so far as they might be helpful in our dialogue. Queer theology offers a pathway to do just that.

THE MEANING OF SEX

This brings us back to the fact that we cannot address questions of sexual intercourse without addressing questions of sex and gender, purpose and meaning – and it is to this latter element which we now turn. Meaning and identity

---

[7] A good example of this in the context of Rwanda is David Bagnall's 'Let's Disagree to Agree: Rwanda and Homosexuality' on the *Via Media* platform: https://viamedia.news/2023/07/04/lets-disagree-to-agree-rwanda-and-homosexuality/ [accessed October 7th 2023].

are closely intertwined, and we must recognise that in the Christian understanding identity is not merely an individual's self-understanding, but a richer and complex dance between the individual, community (or more properly 'communion'), the faith, and God. In matters of sex, gender identity cannot be ignored – as much as those who cling to the vestiges of cis-heteronormativity might like it to be – and hence it is worth exploring that a little further here.

So far, we have focused on the unreal nature of sex categories, and more recently on the similarly unreal nature of homosexuality. It is worth clarifying that it is not the things that they describe that we find to be unreal, but rather the essential categorisation of them, as though those categories have eternal (and theological) value. Identity, however, is something different – and an example of identity would be our gender.[8] Our gender is a mixture of socially derived and individually processed understandings and experiences, and a full discussion of the extremely rich literature in gender studies and queer theory is not possible here. Whilst conservative Christians would go to the barricades over this, a basic ethnographic survey makes it clear that gender identities are not uniform across cultures or across time and adds considerable weight to the need to consider gender identity in matters of sexual intercourse. All that being said, we must also be clear that if our starting point is the individual human person and not the homosexual or heterosexual (or any other unreal category), our paying due attention to that individual diversity also must mean that we pay due attention

---

[8]   The work of Judith Butler on performativity is enormously important in this regard – she argues, for example, that gender is 'a corporeal style, an 'act', as it were', (p.272) suggesting that gender is really an ideology that requires repetition of certain acts in order to retain that status quo, "through language, gesture, and all manner of symbolic social sign" (p.270) (Judith Butler, 'Performative Acts and Gender Constitution: An Essay in Phenomenology and Feminist Theory' in Sue-Ellen Case, ed., *Performing Feminisms: Feminist Critical Theory and Theatre* (Baltimore, MD: Johns Hopkins, 1990). Cis-heteronormativity, in a sense, sets the agenda for our conceptions of gender, and we might argue that escape from this intellectual prison is once again a possible key to our theological enterprise.

to the role of gender in that particular person's experience of the world and lived out sexuality. Once we can meet people as individuals, their particular identity must then surely play a part in our understanding of rightly ordered sexuality – not in a categorising manner nor in a way in which it determines the permissible or the non-permissible, but rather as part of the discernment of the social-sexual life of that individual (and their interaction with their wider milieu).

All of this feeds back into the place of meaning in sexual intercourse. We briefly began a conversation on this in our discussion of casual sex, but it is worth reiterating that sexual intercourse is likely to mean different things to different people, at different times, and with different people – there is no single 'meaning'. The church's immediate response to this has been to try to categorise those different versions of sexual intercourse into a traffic light hierarchical, categorical system of green, amber and red. This simply won't do – it doesn't show even a nod towards the complexity of human life, and also focuses on the mechanics whilst ignoring the intention and the reception (the shared meaning), the individual meaning, and the corporate meaning of each sexual act. In different circumstances, each of these three will be more or less present and – perhaps – relevant, but each surely plays a part in the way in which we might mount a theological engagement with sexual intercourse.

Indeed, it should be becoming clear that to even talk of 'sexual intercourse' as though it were one thing theologically is itself problematic. It is certainly a privileged form of intercourse – it is intimate, or it permits transgression of the intimate – but we must be careful not to over-privilege it in our discussions, and in the process to give it greater import than it can justifiably bear. It sits, then, in that space where it is in many ways more important than we give it credit for and yet not nearly as important as we appear to suggest it is – a comment, perhaps, on the directionality we give that importance, and the helpful and unhelpful orientations from which we approach sex.

Two quite different examples might be engaged with here to illustrate the point, the first amongst them asexuality. Asexual people are no less humanly fulfilled because their sexual-social self is differently construed to the norm (another example of where the norm is a descriptive term and not a prescriptive term). Indeed, in such people we might be tempted to look for a lack rather than for seeking to better understand the way that the sexual might be differently expressed, experienced and engaged with. It is possible, indeed, that the term asexual is itself a misnomer, in that it makes use of categories (sexual, asexual) which themselves are descriptive and cover a deeper complexity that cannot be so simply defined – although, of course, it is not for someone external to that positionality to definitively pronounce on it. What we can say, however, is that asexual people do not have a less intense, less holy, less desirous, less human social existence and ontology – it is simply that their social makeup does not appear to include channelling this through what we would generally regard as the sexual. This is normal human variation and part of God-given diversity.

The other group of people on whom we might reflect are those whose sexual desires pose genuine danger to others, and whose expression of these desires – were it to happen – would be deeply destructive. Because we have jettisoned the unreal categories of sexuality as the basis for rightly ordered sexuality, the importance of consent (including covenanted consent) becomes clearer, without the water being muddied with talk of 'indelicate sexual practices'. For example, there is a clear, unambiguous difference between non-consensual sex and kink, and whilst we may need to think further about the role and nature of consent from a theological perspective (of which more in the next chapter), we must name this truth rather than suggest that all sex outside of covenanted relationship is worthy of equal condemnation (if we would say that it is at all).

It is because sexual intercourse is ultimately an expression of human relating that we must bring ourselves back to interrogating it in that way – taking into account the role of and impact upon the person themselves (both conscious and unconscious, temporal and theological), the partner(s) in that sexual intercourse, the bond, however temporary, that is formed, and the wider social and societal meaning of that sexual intercourse (we see, for example, the importance of the wider meaning in the public nature of covenant).

To return to the Biblical narrative for one moment, it is not at all clear that many (if any) of the Biblical writers could really be said to do justice to the complexity of sexual intercourse (and, indeed, the complexity of gender and sex) if we merely focus on what is said about the mechanics. It is interesting that Jesus' own words on sex (of which there are very few) focus on the relating and not on the doing. Our endless determination to find answers to the questions we ask within the Bible rather than our willingness to allow the Bible to set the terms of the conversation is no surprise when we recognise how the preformed lens of normativity already colours our Biblical approach. The Bible has much to say about sexual intercourse – it is just that we are looking in the wrong places, asking the wrong questions and failing to appreciate that the place where we are likely to learn about this most human of human attributes is in the Biblical narrative about human relating, human flourishing, and the integrated nature of human life.

Were we to appreciate this, then we would draw from the deep and rich well of theological reflection on precisely these questions, and in doing so offer a vision of the sexual self to the world that would be more than worth listening to. The church and the scriptures have much to say about the human person – the person as individual, yet as relating individual, and as relating individual in community – but both the church and the scriptures need to be freed from the prison of normativity – both need to be queered if their potential is to be realised. It is only by seeing sexual intercourse in this way that the church's ideas of sin and grace, holiness, sanctification, redemption and forgiveness can really speak.

7

QUEERING ... THE UNDERSTANDING OF SEX

Why exactly do Christians care about sex?

In recent years, there has been so much noise about penetrative anal sex primarily between consenting men that the wider questions around sexual 'propriety' have fallen somewhat by the wayside. In discussions over same-sex, same-gender marriage, much has been made of the argument that sex must be within heterosexual marriage, with vague gestures towards scripture to justify this, yet very little has been said beyond what is ultimately a fairly reductive approach. If the Christian approach to sex is simply that it must be in 'man and woman' marriage, it is unsurprising that we have so little to say to those for whom the fundamentals of that statement do not hold.

It is the contention of this book that we ought to be spending rather more time thinking and ultimately talking about 'good' sex and 'bad' sex in a way that takes the reality of embodied experience seriously. We ought to do so because sexual intercourse is a key part of human relating, and because our faith – and the scriptures – speak to this wholeness of the human person. Yet as Christians, we are often presented as people who are prudishly and somewhat bizarrely over-interested in this particular facet of human existence. Amongst many in our conservative churches, there is a desire to present a deep conservatism about sex as a single historical thread in

Christianity, but this is simply not the case.[1] In recent debates, indeed, the 'proper' context for sexual intercourse has become (quite literally) part of some more extreme evangelical groups' professions of faith,[2] taking on an almost creedal authority. Arguments are made that this is part of the 'doctrine' of the church, especially the Church of England, with very little working out to show why (or indeed whether) that is the case. Those who disagree with this are labelled unorthodox and – with a lack of charity that would make the Inquisition blush – 'false teachers' and 'wolves in sheep's clothing'.

It is interesting that so much of this 'orthodoxy' hangs on what is little more than implication. There is nowhere in scripture that we can safely say that Jesus explicitly states that sex outside of marriage is wrong. That is not to say that Jesus doesn't speak about the importance of fidelity to the marriage bed, or that St Paul doesn't speak of the importance of good sexual behaviour – both of these things are (most likely) true, and St Paul doubtless speaks of the importance of marriage to sex. Yet on that fundamental question – that sex is for marriage only – so much of what we argue 'but the Bible says' requires our interpretative lenses to be placed on before we approach it.

Now that is not – emphatically not – to suggest that it is not possible to read the scriptures with particular lenses and come to that view. It is doubtless essential that the first-century Jewish contexts of Paul and Jesus are taken into account when we are trying to understand what they are saying about sexual morality, and the assumptions and implications that they themselves would expect their initial hearers to share. Yet similarly, we cannot simply assume that the sexual relationships of today are the same as the sexual relationships of the Biblical

[1]   Diarmaid MacCulloch's 2015 BBC television series, 'Sex and the Church' is a good place to start in this regard, and his forthcoming book, *Sex and the Church: a History*, due to be published by Penguin UK in Autumn 2024, will surely add much to an area which has traded in mistruths for far too long.
[2]   For example that of the Church of England Evangelical Council, available here: https://ceec.info/basis-of-faith/ [accessed October 7th 2023].

eras – as we have argued a number of times to date. We must, therefore, be very careful when we approach the scriptural writing on rightly ordered sexuality, not only to approach it in its own context (which will also require us to recognise the contingency of our understanding) but also to then recognise the challenges of applying such a vastly different contextual understanding of sex and sexuality to the relationships (in the light of our developments in understanding of sex, sexuality, and so on) of our own day.

Much, then, relies on the translation of the word *porneia*, and its use (and intended meaning) by both Paul and Jesus when referring to sexual impropriety. Unfortunately, of course, this word was not actually used by Jesus, given he was likely not speaking in Greek – thus the use of the word *porneia* when referring to Jesus' own words is itself already an act of translation.[3] Whilst it would be more comfortable for conservative theologians were the word more easily definable (and defined), and many make a valiant attempt to pretend that it is so, this is not the case. At the very most, Jesus' cultural context may be suggestive of what he means when (not) using the word, but this is rather shaky ground on which to build such a 'clear' teaching. *Porneia* remains a word whose specific meaning is both general and contextual, and hence if we wish to read particular meanings into it in its Biblical place, then it is easy to do so. Of course, this means that if the Bible is read through the cis-heteronormative lens, then *porneia* becomes increasingly easy to define![4]

---

[3] And contextualisation – in that our deduced translation needs to be read within the context of contemporary thinking and writing.

[4] This is a key point. Interpretative decisions are already being made when we approach scriptural writing on *porneia*, meaning that we end up in a rather circular argument. This highlights the difficulty with divine command ethics – briefly, that a list of right and wrong (particularly in terms of acts) can be easily read from scripture. This is a tempting way of approaching the Bible, but it Is not an honest one, because it fails to take into account the way we derive the meaning of particular words (for example 'sexual immorality' or 'lust', as we will discuss). We can all agree sexual immorality is wrong – it's immoral – but we cannot necessarily agree on what the Bible is (variously) calling sexual immorality.

Yet if we approach the text without these preconceptions, it is by no means clear that *porneia* is primarily referring to particular acts – indeed, it is much more likely to be referring to a stance of sexual immorality more generally. Here then, of course, we come full circle – it is clear that there is Biblical interest in avoiding sexual immorality, yet no very clear description of what that might mean in terms of specific acts. We are drawn back to sex and sexuality being part of the entire human person rather than a separate element. We care about sexual 'immorality' because it impacts on the wider morality of the individual – to put that in another way, we care about the sexual self because it is not separable from the wider self.

Of course, it is also important that we are not naïve when approaching Paul's writing. It is certainly the case that he appears to place an emphasis on sexual propriety in terms of social propriety – and once again we must take into account the context in which he is writing, and the accusations of sexual impropriety that will be levelled against the early Christians (and, indeed, the wish to distinguish and delineate Christian households from the pagan, including in matters of sexual behaviour). Yet here again, we must be careful not to suggest that the end results that Paul comes to are the same as his reasoning – he is not free of assumptions or particular context, and nor should we pretend that he is. Thus, whilst it is important to engage with Paul's theological arguments about the human person, we must be careful not to see this in continuity with applying particular practical and applied conclusions determined in a particular place, time, and socio-cultural context, in a universal way.

Before we turn to the various out-workings of sex, it is worth recognising that the previous few paragraphs do sound dangerously like apologetics! Yet we must also be clear that we cannot simply ignore the Biblical record – we must engage with it, and a queer approach allows us to do so in a way that helps us to remove the lenses we might otherwise try to place (or find others placing for us). We present this very brief introduction to these Biblical arguments because for too long there has been a narrative that there is a clear and unambiguous Biblical argument that sex outside of (heterosexual) marriage is condemned – yet it is abundantly clear that this is not the case. Queer readings of scripture are anything but unorthodox – instead, they help us to really get to grips with what the Bible says rather than what we might prefer that it said.

Hence, we can indeed say that sexual behaviour matters. God is interested in us – loves us – as full, integrated persons, and hence we cannot simply isolate sexuality off and either suggest it is unimportant or conversely argue that it is judged (and hence ordered) differently from all other forms of human behaviour and interaction.[5] Sexual immorality is not its own, boxed off region of our lives which has no bearing on anything else – it is just as integrated into our whole self as our other ways of relating with God, other people, and the created order. It is on these terms that we should engage with it.

ENGAGING WITH SEX

It should be clear by now that sexual intercourse and discussions around it are anything but simple! We will attempt to think through the different 'expressions' of sexual intercourse, yet in doing so we ought to be wary of attempts to form discrete categories of sexual expression (for example, casual, committed, etc). It is of the nature of queer theology that any attempt at categorisation should be treated with

---

[5] As we saw in *Queer Holiness*, on matters of sexuality and gender there is overwhelming evidence from the human and social sciences against the conservative position, in stark contrast to so much else that is debated in theology where these different sources align. It remains curious that on matters of sexuality and gender, this evidence on human flourishing is so willingly and entirely ignored in the name of 'Biblical truth', which we have shown here and there to be an unsafe assertion.

great suspicion, and hence we might at this stage simply say that whilst we might be able to speak of sexual intercourse occurring within particular bounds (for example, within covenanted relations), not all sex within those bounds will be of a particular type, and indeed that is not simply a factor of poor moral behaviour but rather a recognition of the complexity of human life. For example, sex between a married couple will not necessarily always be procreative (using the wider meaning of the term below) in nature, and the complexity of the interaction between the relationship, the individual and the particular sexual expression will itself speak to the 'intercourse' undertaken.

It is of the nature of something physical expressing something ontological that such conversations are complex – far more complex than the puerile debate in too many church circles permits. The suggestion that 'sex is for marriage only' not only ignores this complexity, but also appears to make pretence that these different facets of sexual expression do not exist. Once we are able to recognise these different facets, we can rightly have a conversation about how these might tie into different forms of relationship – whether that be friendship, covenant (or marriage), and so on. However, it is not possible to do so by using the Bible as an instruction manual, not least because it does not answer these questions. We are addressing issues of sexual morality, which appears to be a Biblical mandate, yet we are not given simplistic answers to denote behaviour in terms of sexual acts. The sources of scripture, tradition, reason and experience are doubtless important in engaging theologically in this area, however much the argument has been made that the Bible is 'clear' – it objectively is not.

SEX WITH GOD

As we have mentioned, sexual intercourse has an impact on the people involved and whatever relationship there might be between them. However, it is also important to recognise that sexual intercourse has been traditionally associated with desire for God as well. Before turning to the forms of sex in the way they might impact on human relationship, it is worth drawing attention to this and exploring it a little further. At the heart of this conversation is the place of desire – and rightly ordered desire – and the extent to which it lies behind rightly ordered sexuality.[6] Desire for God, as the eschatological endpoint of the human orientation, is thus seen as the endpoint of all human desire – in other words, all human desires are ultimately reflections of or contributions to the desire of human beings for God (which itself may be a reflection of the desire of God for human beings).

It can thus be argued that sexual desire is a particularly human way of expressing desire not only for the other, but for the Other – for God – through that desire for the other. Sexual intimacy is then a reflection of intimacy with God, and therefore our sexual desires should be consonant with desire for God rather than in opposition to it. Once again, whilst we can see why the constructions of cis-heteronormativity have been used to declare same-sex or same-gender desire as being in opposition to this desire for God, when we approach sex and sexuality as part of the God given human nature that is poured out on all humanity, we would more rightly recognise that forbidding that desire without good cause would itself be an attempted infringement of the desire for the Other. Of course, not all human desires are good (sexual or otherwise), but our recognition that they need to be consonant with desire for God means that our starting point requires us to interrogate those desires as they are, as opposed to fitting them into an arbitrary ideological framework and limiting our willingness to ask questions of them.

As we have noted previously, there have been attempts to instil a certain dualism into our understanding of the human

---

[6] There is much that cannot be included here for reasons of space, but readers may wish to engage with Augustine and his detractors on this in the first instance!

person in matters of sexuality, most particularly in the way that queer people have been loved as 'sinner' whilst 'sin' is hated. This flesh-spirit dualism is fundamentally unchristian – our desire and our action is ultimately not something separable in the truest sense, although again we must be clear that to desire does not necessarily mean that one must act on that desire. An act borne from desire, however, is a reflection of that desire,[7] and hence the issue lies with the desire itself rather than with the act, and this takes on particular importance when the desire is not merely for human intimacy but really a reflection for divine intimacy. Our focus must be, then, on the desire and the relationship between the desire and the act. This is complex in, for example, casual sex – but in this situation, it is clear that it is primarily the desire that needs to be interrogated rather than the sexual act itself. The sexual act is one of enacted meaning – and hence the same act may represent a different meaning, even within the same individual. Whether those different meanings can both reflect desire for God but in different ways is something we will return to in our discussions of non-covenant sexual intercourse below.

SEX AS PROCREATION

A point to which we must now turn is the bringing up of children. So far, we have primarily looked at relationality from the perspective of the individuals directly involved in the relationship itself, and we might rightly be hauled up as having completely ignored the products of reproduction that such relationships – on occasion – introduce! There is not the space to do this issue full justice, but it is right to note it here and make clear that it needs to be taken into account

---

[7] Hence the importance of actively understanding and confronting desires, whatever their moral positioning. *Queer Holiness* touches on some of the psychological defence mechanisms we use in this process.

in any conversation about relationships in which children are included, whether as the biological children of the parents or as adoptive children. Once again, far too much is said in this area that relies on half-truths or misquoted statistics, and we must be careful to ensure that whatever psychological evidence (for example) we quote to help us determine the best (itself an unhelpfully loaded term) place for the bringing up of children is actually accurate.

Children, as a possible but not essential consequence of procreation, are surely in many ways front and centre in a discussion of any relationship from which they are to be nurtured, and it may be that the introduction of children into the equation changes some of our other calculations and considerations. That said, what we have said about cis-heteronormativity pertains here – 'every child must have a father and a mother' is borne primarily out of ideology than out of evidence, and we need to do the theological work to determine what the right form of relationship might be to provide the best for parents and children alike. Thus, it may add complexity into the situation, but does not fundamentally change the way in which we might engage with the questions raised.

This might appear a rather brief discussion of children given their usual centrality to many of the conversations of marriage, and we may ask whether there is something fundamentally different in relationships which feature children compared to those which do not. This question, once again, needs to be engaged with theologically, taking into account all the evidence we might be able to garner from our different theological sources. Robert Song,[8] in his discussion of procreation (of which more below), suggests that there is something materially different between relationships which do and don't contain children, and reserves the name marriage for those which do (or might). Whether we agree with him will

---

[8] Robert Song, *Covenant and Calling: Towards a Theology of Same-Sex Relationships* (London: SCM Press, 2014)

rest in no small part on our understanding of procreation.

Indeed, for many who oppose same-sex, same-gender marriage and yet who recognise that there may be a place for sexual intimacy in such couples (which appears to be the view of the Church of England's House of Bishops), the opposition to calling such covenanted relationships 'marriage' is their lack of openness to procreation. We have previously touched on the potentially homophobic nature of this objection (given, for example, marriage post hysterectomy), and we will not engage in further discussions here as to whether what is really being discussed in the Church of England actually goes beyond semantics. However, we will now turn to the meaning of procreation and ask whether it is truly synonymous with reproduction.

Sex as reproduction is not something we need address here in much detail, except to recognise that we cannot simply dismiss this out of hand nor can we call it the only (or even typical) male-female expression of sexuality. Sex between men and women of a particular age bracket is usually (although not always, by any means) open to a reproductive function, and it is certainly the case that one element of procreation is reproduction. However, this is by no means the only element. In its truest sense, pro-creation is ultimately a participation in the creative activity of God, at God's invitation, oriented towards the ends that God has 'in mind', and not those we want to impose upon God. Procreation is something we are invited into, not something we do – and this being the case, there is very good reason indeed for us to find procreative purposes and lifegiving blessings in queer sexuality.

In his discussion of creation in *Radical Love*, Patrick Cheng describes 'unmerited self-giving love' as being 'at the heart of all forms of committed relationships, not procreation', by which he means reproduction. He argues that 'just as creation is an act of pure grace on the part of God, so is procreation', and that 'creation is much more than God's affirmation of procreation'. He goes on to say:

> Creation is about the radical love that spills out of the Trinity and overflows into the created order. God brings us into existence as a result of pure grace. As such, God's grace is at the heart of the doctrine of creation, and queer relationships bear witness to such grace.[9]

To this, we must surely answer 'Amen', yet we must also surely be more willing to challenge the meaning of the word procreation on Cheng's own terms. 'Just as creation is an act of pure grace … so is procreation' is entirely true – yet it is not at all clear why this 'procreation' should be restricted to simply reproduction in this case. Procreation in its wider meaning – participation in the creative activity and will of God – is also an act of pure grace, and hence 'creation is much more than God's affirmation of' **reproduction** (replacing Cheng's procreation) gives a much fuller and richer reading. Procreation understood in this way is our participation in the 'radical love that spills out', and queer relationships 'bear witness to such grace' in the fact that they are themselves procreative.

This may appear to be an argument of semantics, but it is of utmost importance when we approach questions of marriage, its nature as a 'gift of God in creation', and the definitional association of procreation with such a relationship. Our human understanding of procreation has indeed been widened – we see the pro-creative in adoption, in the nurturing of families and communities, in the outpouring of grace that is not merely constrained to reproduction, and yet which is indeed present in this particular participation in God's creative power. Reproduction is, then, a particular form of procreation but it is not the only form – and queer relationships are living examples of this being the case. The Genesis narrative (and indeed the wider scriptural narrative, most particularly that found in the Epistles) is not *merely* about multiplication of

[9] Patrick Cheng, *Radical Love*, p. 67

humans but about their nurture, about the growing of the Kingdom of God, and about the importance of spiritual growth (the enriching of society and strengthening of community described in the Common Worship Marriage Preface).[10] It is all of this that procreation, most particularly in the light of the incarnation, death and resurrection of Christ, surely contains (as we shall meet in the next chapter's discussion of Robert Song's argument).

To return to sexual expression, then, we can recognise the procreative role of sexual intercourse in humankind generally, rather than in a sense that excludes the queer. Considering the interplay between *forms* of relationship (for example, the covenanted and the casual) and *expressions* of sexual intercourse, we might reasonably generally associate the procreative with the covenantal – that is, we might see sexual expression within covenanted relationships serving a procreative purpose in a way that we might not see as much in other relationships (although this may not be a neatly formed Venn diagram). This suggests that the form of relationship impacts on the nature of the sexual expression, even if this is not the only factor. Thus we might say that covenantal relationships enable sex to be more procreative in nature, and procreation increases their covenantal nature, one building up the other. That this is the case in queer relationships in the same way as any other relationship is hardly a matter for debate.

In addition to this outward-facing procreative aspect, we might also argue that procreation also has an inward-facing aspect, the building up of relationships. In many ways this should not be a surprise, and reflects much of the understanding of sexual expression in marriage. The Book of Common Prayer expresses one of the purposes of marriage as follows:

[10] The Church of England, *Marriage*, available here: https://www. churchofengland.org/prayer-and-worship/worship-texts-and-resources/ common-worship/marriage [accessed October 7th 2023].

It was ordained for the mutual society, help, and comfort, that the one ought to have of the other, both in prosperity and adversity.

The Alternative Preface for the Marriage service in Common Worship makes clear the role of sexual intercourse in this process:

It [marriage] is given, that with delight and tenderness they may know each other in love, and, through the joy of their bodily union, may strengthen the union of their hearts and lives.

Traditionally, we may have thought of these two roles of sex as distinct, but perhaps we might see them as the particular covenantal expression of procreativity – a creativity both inwards for the relationship and the people involved, and outwards for the relationship and those whom the goods of the relationship impact upon. To bring us back to sexual intercourse, we might rightly say that the intercourse here is procreative, but the particular sexual acts that are involved are somewhat immaterial to the meaning of the intercourse. Whether penetrative, non-penetrative, overtly sexual, or indeed simply an expression of the sexual-social, this intercourse is one of building up and creative participation.

It is important to caveat this, because we know that certain acts are entirely outside of the realm of lifegiving sexuality. It is primarily the intention behind these acts, and their reception, which makes them unacceptable – we might think here first and foremost of consent, but also of the bounds of that consent (in terms of what is being consented to). It is a truism that non-consensual sexual activity is wrong, and this is not only because of the impact that this has on the physical but also on the psychological and more – it is not going too far to suggest that it is wrong because of its being an assault on the ontological, an invasion of a space which can only rightly be freely given because it is of that person's essential nature. The non-consensual must surely wound the active perpetrator, too – not in a way that is remotely comparable to the hurt experienced by the victim, but nonetheless in a theologically important manner.

Whilst there has been a recognition of the importance of consent in ecclesial conversations around sex and sexuality in recent years, the sad reality is that this is not something that has been frequently steeped in theological understanding, and more often than not Christianity and some of her proponents have appeared entirely on the wrong side in discussions of sexual consent (for example in debates around marital rape). The church is so used to blaming the world for sexual licentiousness that it appears unable or unwilling to remove the plank from its own eye when it surveys its own history. Consent is very clearly a theological imperative, yet there remains far too little discussion within the Christian church of what consent means and what the ramifications of this are for our conversations around sex. In many ways, consent appears to be the key player in any conversation around sex and sexual ethics.

Yet we cannot leave our conversation about sexual expression here. Whilst we have spoken about procreative sex in covenantal terms, we must also recognise that such covenanted relationship is not the only place that sexual expression takes place. As we have stated before (and as the Bishop of Dover made clear at the General Synod of the Church of England), this is not merely happening amongst queer people – it is happening amongst people, period, young and old, including large numbers of Christians, including clergy. Whilst official church teaching has been (and remains) to say that sex is for marriage only, we have shown in these pages the inadequacy of this being presented in the simplistic way that it normally is. We might, instead, now argue that the church should teach that sex is for covenanted relationships only, an argument that might be based on this sexual intercourse being of a procreative nature. That leads us to ask whether that argument truly holds – and whether it holds because of an underlying theological truth rather than simply prejudice.

CASUAL SEX

The phrase 'casual sex' has appeared several times to date in this book, and has much cultural purchase, yet can refer to a multitude of different forms of sexual expression outside of romantic relationship. It may involve a single sexual encounter with a stranger, either as a one-off anonymous encounter or after a brief social engagement – the former may happen in a sex club where neither individual can even see the other (for example in a dark room). Casual sex might also refer to sex between friends ('friends with benefits'), sex between work colleagues, sex with 'no emotional involvement' (on its own terms), swinging, social sex in a group (possibly but not solely in the context of drugs) – and more besides.

Whilst such sexual encounters are described as non-romantic, that is not the same as saying there is no intimacy – indeed, whilst there may be different shades of intimacy, nonetheless these forms of sex should include a form of consent which permits entry into a social-sexual place that is by its nature intimate. Indeed, the experience of intimacy in such encounters may in fact be heightened compared to some covenantal relationships because of the intentional choice of each encounter on each occasion (although this is by no means always the case, and perhaps rests on an understanding of intimacy as passionate eroticism that does not take into account the potential for deepening intimacy in life-long partnerships, and the multi-faceted nature of intimacy itself).[11]

Thus, whilst the intention of such sexual encounters is to focus on the individual experience of the one entering into such encounters rather than the relationship between two (or more) people, the dividing line is clearly not between romantic and intimate, but rather between something which

[11] We have previously made mention of the psychological impact of casual sex. This cannot be ignored and must surely be factored into our conversations. However, it is not at all clear that a one-size-fits-all model applies.

is intended and received as romantic, and something which is intended and received as 'casual'. Of note, the intention and the reception may not align, even if the purpose and nature of the sexual encounter has been explicitly agreed upon beforehand, not least because of the potential for any intimate act to be open to the development of romantic feeling. It is hard, then, despite the best of intentions of both parties to be sure that 'casual sex' will remain just that, and the basket of anecdotal evidence overflows to suggest that this is by no means always the case. This intimacy, the impact of its being shared, and the interpretation (or, indeed, misinterpretation) of this sharing is surely of theological import.

This willing sharing of and in intimate space also makes it less clear that arguments against 'casual sex' from the perspective of objectification of others hold much weight. All sexual encounters, whether romantic or otherwise, contain within themselves something of the willing self-objectification and of the objectification of the other – a desiring for the other, and yet also a receptivity of the desire of the other to and in one's own person. Our unfortunate characterisation of all 'unmarried' sexual desire as lust is a short cut, but a poor one that doesn't do justice to either the scriptural text or lived experience.[12] Thus, whilst we can see that Jesus' oft-quoted teaching on lust (Matthew 5:27-30) is of course in some way relevant to our

---

[12] It is interesting that the words we translate as 'lust' in the Scriptures have themselves already been interpretatively processed – in other words, what exactly do we mean by 'lust', and why? Whilst we hear much about 'lust' applying to anyone who feels sexual excitement towards another person, it is not at all clear that 'lust', as Biblically described, can be so easily extricated from its embeddedness within relationality. Indeed, to return to our theme in Chapter 4, there is a convincing case that 'lust' is actually *primarily* referring to a fissure of relationship (hence lust within marriage) rather than to sex *per se*. However, because of historical associations of lust with sexual desire, we end up in a place where we fail to listen to the actual words and meaning of Scripture. Once again, we meet our presenting issue – that the way we read scripture in a church context is often unconsciously impacted by the lenses we place on it. Cis-heteronormativity can only gain from such a position, as can our obsession with respectability and propriety. We must get better at asking the searching questions about what the words we use *actually mean*, and how we derive this meaning.

discussions of sexual continency and objectification, we can also see that its context is that of adultery and covenantal relationship, and not necessarily a *tout court* rejection of sexual desire, most particularly outside of such a covenant.[13]

Yet to make things even more complicated, it is by no means absolute that procreative sex is only to be found in covenantal relationship – or, indeed, it may be that there are different forms of covenant *in situ* here, whereby each 'casual sexual' encounter is itself experienced within a short-lived but extant covenant between two people, in which the relating between the couple is both selfishly yet also selflessly directed towards each individual's experiencing the moment of sexual pleasure and intimacy rather than in a romantic connection. In this case, the intimacy is a shared relational experience and each is offering up their own social-sexual intimate space for the other to enjoy for mutual benefit, yet not for lasting relationship (hence finding a better definition in covenant than contract). Whether this can truly be called procreative is a matter for debate, yet it may be that the intimacy shared does fulfil the grounds such as freedom of choice to share with others and an act of free grace. What is clear is that relationships such as marriage might be better described as long-lasting covenant rather than merely covenantal, given the role of free choice and the openness of intimate space in these 'casual' sexual experiences.

PROCREATION AND PLEASURE

This all leads us to ask whether, in fact, all sex is procreative – and just as importantly, whether all sex needs to be so.

[13]   A rejection of such a *tout court* attitude means that we need to find other ways to discuss the appropriate place of sexual desire in the lives of both those in covenant and those outside. Perhaps here we might think of such questions in terms of aesthetics, temperance, negotiation, and honesty, rather than the pretence that too often builds up when 'lust' becomes a catch-all word that apparently condemns all sexual desire as somehow ungodly.

A further question might be whether there are somehow grades of procreativity, and if so whether 'good' sex must find itself above an (arbitrary) barrier in this gradated scale. Is what we are really interested in whether sex is building up an *erotic romantic relationship* only, and if so, why? Is it possible that sex might also be used successfully to build up non-romantic relationships, and if so, is this a problem theologically? Is sex as social pastime something that should be entirely forbidden by the church, and – once again – if so, why? What is it about active sexual continency *in general* that we think is so important (as opposed to continency of sexual desire, which we know to be impossible in the human state, however much we might try to repress it)?

We need to be able to defend such assertions theologically if we are to make them – and this defence needs to be stronger than vague references to marriage or arguments built on disgust, propriety, or 'it's not for me so it shouldn't be for anyone'. Similarly, the church needs to grow up in its discussions of alternative sexual practices, including kink, fetish, the use of sex toys, and similar, recognising not only that these are enjoyed by many outside the queer community as well as within it, but might also be enjoyed by those who are in committed, exclusive, covenanted relationships as well. For too long, queer people have been scapegoated for what appears to be little more than squirming, squeamish, prudish discomfort about sex practices outside the norm, and yet there is very little theologically defensible in such opposition.

Exactly what is wrong with (for example) genuinely consensual BDSM sexual practices or foot fetishism within cis-heterosexual marriage (to take the most conservative example) is extremely hard to decipher, and yet there apparently remains 'Christian opposition' to such practices. Whilst we may wish to interrogate the directionality of desire, there is nothing obviously intrinsically unchristian about sexual desire being expressed for an unconventional encounter with the other *per se* (unconventional, and yet likely entirely within the bounds of normal human behaviour). Of course, there may be important questions about the directionality of desire and its psychological (and theological) impact in certain kinks – for example, the need (rather than preference) for degradation in the sexual encounter, which may reflect a genuinely unhealthy approach to sexuality that does damage. In this sense, the impact of all sexual expressions is not equal, but what matters is the questions we ask, which are not about the expression so much as what it signifies and acts out, and how it impacts on those involved.

Of course, some kink involves paraphilia (sexual desire enhanced by or directed towards objects rather than people). In some cases, paraphilias (and sex toys) are nonetheless associated with sexual intercourse with another – they are an addition to this sexual experience, and whilst we may question the psychological health associated with such paraphilias[14] it is hard to argue that they are particularly theologically questionable if they can form part of a healthy sexual expression. Yet even for those paraphilias which do not involve relationality with others, nonetheless we must be careful that we do not mistake the psychological for the theological (although, of course, the theological must take account of the psychological). Thus, whilst we may wish to ask about the directionality of the desire and the compatibility of this with desire for God, outright condemnation of such practices is by no means the only Christian response.

Such a perspective becomes clearer when we turn to the case of masturbation (which may be the form of sexual expression in such cases). It remains fascinating that having a sexual encounter in which there is no 'other' is considered to be of lesser moral guilt than sexual encounter with a

---

[14] They remain, for example, debated as specific 'disorders' in psychiatric communities, for example in the development of the recent ICD-11. Whereas ICD-10 (the European psychiatric diagnostic manual) included paraphilias such as fetishism, in ICD-11, paraphilias that do not involve a lack of consent must include either marked distress to the individual concerned due to the nature of the arousal pattern (and not the rejection by others) or significant risk of injury or death. This casts further light on the relevance (or otherwise) of normativity for mental health diagnosis.

partner of the same sex or gender by many self-described conservative Christians. Whilst some historical arguments against masturbation clearly now hold no weight (for example, those based on the false belief that semen contains the new human life in its entirety, and hence the 'spilling of the seed' means the end of human life), nonetheless it is stark how little is said about the potentially problematic nature of masturbation. Acceptance of masturbation is an acceptance that the sexual climax – whilst being part of all the processes we have outlined in these three chapters – may also on occasion simply be a cause of individual pleasure, a biological process which leads to short term excitement and gratification. That is not to demean it, but to suggest that it can be both that and part of the way that humankind relates to God and one another.

If we do then accept that masturbation is a valid form of sexual expression, then we must surely accept that the sexual expression as release, as unidirectional, as self-centred, as sexual pleasure and as lacking in direct relationality is not only possible but also entirely within the God-given human experience – in other words, climaxing certainly can tend towards building up relationship, but it can also just be a brief act of God-given, individually focused joy (which may or may not be indirectly relational). Masturbation does not offer any form of covenant, direct shared intimacy or relatedness, and may embody the ultimate example of the separation of sexual expression (specifically climax) from any of these.

This may not, of course, always be the case. Indeed, masturbation as an action may be associated with a number of causes of sexual desire or excitement in the masturbator (whether fantasy, pornography (of which more in the following chapter), etc), and the directionality of this desire (to God, to or about others) may itself be the proper subject of theological questions. Masturbation may, in fact, be an extension of relationality – for example it may help (or hinder) relationality within covenantal relationship – a somewhat related example of which might be the concept of virtual sexual intimacy without touch (i.e. sexting, video-call masturbation, of which more in the next chapter).

However, if we do accept masturbation, then it is also hard to determine why such sexual expression should be restricted to the individual in a closed room. There seems little material difference (beyond negotiations of the intimate space) between masturbation alone or alongside another, and similarly little material difference again between this and mutual masturbation or sexual activity with another purely for the purposes of sexual release. The dividing line between this kind of sexual activity and the short-term covenantal is not at all clear, and logically perhaps the only difference between sole masturbation and such sexual activity with another is the inclusion of the other, who by virtue of this inclusion brings a relational and possibly covenantal element with them.

CONCLUSION

This suggests that, as we come full circle, the categorical differences that we wish to impose upon sexuality ultimately break down, even if they might hold some descriptive purpose. We are left with themes of consent, covenant, procreation, relating, and pleasure, each of which is found within the diversity of experience that forms humankind's encounter with the sexual. Much has been written about all of these, but it remains clear that consent as a theological virtue and theological impetus requires much more engagement from theologians and Christians more widely. Of course, the thrust of this chapter has not been that every permutation of sex in each of the situations outlined would correctly be called 'rightly ordered', but rather that our attempts at categorisation in this way is itself a futile exercise. We might think, for example, of whether sex work is truly consent freely given or covenantal in nature (it appears to fit a more contractual paradigm), and hence whether it falls within the forms of sexuality that are rightly ordered.[15]

If we are searching for the categorical, then it is really only at consent that our various sources of knowledge and understanding converge – the intimate requires consent for it to be in any way godly. Consent, hospitality, and holiness are closely related, and there is much more to be said about these. For now, however, let us turn to the ways our developed narrative of relating and the sexual-social might play out in the life of the church and its institutions. There is surely no better place to start than marriage.

---

[15] Of note, whilst we might indeed argue that sex work is not rightly ordered sexuality, this is a long way from condemning those whose circumstances lead them to this way of earning a living. Unfortunately, because of the way that the church has historically spoken about sex, this message has been entirely lost – and rather too often, not even transmitted in the first place. This topic deserves a book in its own right, but we must surely consider the impact of paying for sex in terms of the intercourse, the people involved, and wider society. For example, can and should intimacy ever be bought and sold, or does this falling short of the idea of covenant create an insurmountable barrier? Should sexual intercourse always be covenantal in some form? Is our reticence about sex work based on a discomfort with paying for pleasure which includes the intimate? How does this relate to questions of paid-for pornography or sex phone lines? How might we couch this for those whose only option for sexual experience might be paid-for (for whatever reason)? This is, perhaps, an extreme example of an unequal power differential which itself appears to run contrary to properly ordered sexual intimacy and intercourse, and itself casts questions on genuinely free consent.

PART III
QUEERING OUR LIVES

8

QUEERING ... MARRIAGE

We started this book with a not entirely enthusiastic view of the benefits of discussing marriage! As we move into this part of our conversation where we think about whether what we have explored might make a material difference to the way we look, behave, and engage with the world as a church, it is only because we have undertaken this thinking that we are able to re-engage with this particular element of the Christian life. Marriage is not the be all and end all – and nor should it be the starting point for our exploration of queer sexuality. Marriage is, instead, a place that we find our doctrine and theology worked out – as the church suggests, in sacramental terms.

It is for this reason that what follows is not an apologetic argument. It is not the purpose of this chapter to argue that, or even why, non-cis-heterosexuals should be permitted into the marriage bed. To those who have followed our argument so far, it should be abundantly clear that the only opposition remaining to such a position is cis-heteronormative ideology, and yet it should also be clear that simply strong-arming queer people into an unchanged cis-heteronormative institution is deeply unsatisfactory, not only for those queer people but for our understanding of marriage itself. What we will ask here, then, is not whether such people *can* get married, but instead given the fact that they self-evidently *are* married, what can this tell us about the institution of marriage *per se*.

We will address the elephant in the room more widely

in a moment but let us touch on it briefly here – much to the surprise of the cis-heteronormative gatekeepers found in so many churches, many queer people quite simply aren't interested in entering into such a flawed and stained institution. Queer people, including many Christians, may quite rightly say at this point – but we are not interested in getting married, and our relationships are most certainly not the same as cis-heteronormative marriage – and we thank God for it! Our relationships are not burdened with the baggage of marriage, with the deeply unchristian parts of its history and indeed its present, and we have no need for it. There is much to commend in this, yet nonetheless, there is a benefit in teasing out if there is anything to save from this much flawed institution. Is there anything that married relationships, whatever we might call them, do or could particularly reflect of the love and relationship of God (hence, for example, suggesting that they are Sacrament rather than merely sacramental)?

We will continue to navigate this tension as we move throughout this chapter. Queerness brings with it a much needed hermeneutic of suspicion when approaching marriage, and yet it is not totally clear that the institution is entirely beyond redemption. Here, then, is our first quest of queer redemption – where queerness can not only challenge but refine, and where it allows us to live in the land of uncertainty, contingency, and questioning, and to find that land to be a theologically fertile one.

MARRIAGE AS SACRAMENT

Before we go further, and to lay out the case for the defence of marriage as an institution, we must engage with the idea of marriage as sacrament. There have been many definitions of these through Christian history, focusing on their role as 'outward and visible signs of an inward and spiritual grace'. Andrew Davison describes them as such:

> The sacraments are actions, often humble, through which God works and acts upon us. They are everything that we are, and purposefully so: physical, material, speaking, cultural ... The sacraments are occasions when we encounter Christ.[1]

This encountering of Christ suggests that when the sacraments are celebrated there is something very particular being communicated and manifested about the life of God, and the life of God's people – in other words, sacraments are a particular window – yet an efficacious one – into the life and work of the Spirit. Following on from our discussions in Part 2, it is surely also the case that the sacraments speak of – and allow a particular participation in – the relationality of God. Marriage, therefore, has worth as a sacrament not because it mysteriously descended from heaven at some point in human history but because the church recognises something of this efficacious window onto the divine in the joining together into 'one flesh' of two people (historically understood as being one man and one woman).

Our key question might therefore be what precisely it is that the church recognises as embodying this 'efficacious window' in this particular scenario. Through Christian history, from Augustine to the present day, this question has been front and centre, and yet too often the answer has been placed in the suffocating frame of cis-heteronormativity, preventing any serious reflection on the fact that what is being referred to are human goods that can be displayed in a relationship in which the gender of sex or the participants is immaterial.

The Common Worship liturgy of the Church of England puts it like this (which has some continuity with, but different emphasis than that from which it springs in the Book of

---

[1] Andrew Davison, *Why Sacraments?* (Westmont, IL: InterVarsity, 2013) p.1. Readers will find this a rich and helpful reflection on the role of sacraments in the church today that seeks to engage with their essence and not their periphery.

Common Prayer, and which also has significant commonality with the marriage rites of other denominations):[2]

> *Marriage is a gift of God in creation*
> *through which husband and wife may know the grace*
> *of God.*
>
> *It is given*
> *that as man and woman grow together in love and*
> *trust,*
> *they shall be united with one another in heart, body*
> *and mind,*
> *as Christ is united with his bride, the Church.*
>
> *The gift of marriage brings husband and wife together*
> *in the delight and tenderness of sexual union*
> *and joyful commitment to the end of their lives.*
> *It is given as the foundation of family life*
> *in which children are [born and] nurtured*
> *and in which each member of the family,*
> *in good times and in bad,*
> *may find strength, companionship and comfort,*
> *and grow to maturity in love ...*
>
> *Marriage is a sign of unity and loyalty*
> *which all should uphold and honour.*
> *It enriches society and strengthens community.*

Whilst arguments continue between different denominations (and indeed within them) about whether marriage is to be recognised as a sacrament or as merely sacramental, nonetheless this passage gives an indication as to where the goods of marriage are found and hence the reason that

---

[2] he Church of England, *Marriage*, available here: https://www.churchofengland.org/prayer-and-worship/worship-texts-and-resources/common-worship/marriage [accessed October 7th 2023].

churches, whether accepting marriage as sacramental or otherwise, still wish to call it holy and bless it. Yet in recent years there has been so much noise about the sex or gender of the participants, that banal definitional statements such as 'marriage is between a man and a woman' has trumped the richness of the understanding of the sacrament.

In the Church of England, reference is frequently made to canon law (a set of regulations for the government of the church) by those who oppose same-sex, same-gender marriage, and specifically to Canon B30, which is often described as placing an emphasis on this reference to sex and gender. However, whilst Canon B30 (1) does indeed mention the sex or gender of the participants, this is by no means the only thing it says:

> *The Church of England affirms, according to our Lord's teaching, that marriage is in its nature a union permanent and lifelong, for better for worse, till death them do part, of one man with one woman, to the exclusion of all others on either side, for the procreation and nurture of children,[3] for the hallowing and right direction of the natural instincts and affections, and for the mutual society, help and comfort which the one ought to have of the other, both in prosperity and adversity.*

There is much more here to be discussed than sex or gender, however much it might suit those who see marriage as their possession to focus on these elements. We will return to a discussion of the role of complementarity in this sacramentality later in this chapter, but for now we can see

---

[3] Of note, whilst marriage is said to be the place where children should be brought up, this is not the same as saying every marriage must include children. This casts a rather different light on the necessity (or otherwise) of marriage to include reproduction and the bringing up of children. Just because marriage is said to be the place it should happen does not mean that the happening of it is essential for something to be called marriage. We have engaged with this from a number of directions throughout our argument, but it is worth stating this clearly here.

that there is much more to be engaged with here, and in the Preface to the Marriage service, that speaks directly to the question: 'why is marriage a sacrament?'. Queerness, by refocusing on this, can help us regain an understanding of why exactly the church values marriage – and allow us to interrogate whether marriage holds a special place in the exemplification of these elements, whether these elements are themselves truly reflective of the relationality of God, and thus whether marriage can be truly called a sacrament, or indeed more sacramental than other forms of human relationship.

MARRIAGE AS CREATION ORDINANCE

To begin to answer this question, we must turn to the thorny issue of whether marriage is indeed a creation ordinance – and what this might mean. As we have seen, the Preface to the Marriage service in the Church of England contains the words 'marriage is a gift of God in creation', and yet we know from the historical record that it was not until the Council of Trent (1563) that marriage was formally declared a sacrament, and that whilst 'the preface to Trent's canons on marriage seemed to imply that orthodox Christians had always recognised marriage to be "truly and properly" one of the seven sacraments of the New Law ... everyone knew that that was not the case'.[4] Of course, to recognise something as a 'gift of God in creation' is not the same as saying that it was always called such, yet it is also important to recognise that what the church is doing with its co-option of marriage is engaging with a particular form of human relationship, refining and defining what it is about that relationship which makes it sacramental (and, indeed, practice and theory may

---

[4] Philip Reynolds, *How Marriage Became One of the Sacraments: The Sacramental Theology of Marriage from its Medieval Origins to the Council of Trent* (Cambridge: CUP, 2016) p.4

not have been much more than extremely loosely aligned through much of its history), and then subsuming that form of relationship into the teaching of the church.

Marriage is then, at heart, a recognition of the holiness of a covenanted state.[5] We might be tempted in a world where people go to church to 'get married' to believe that it is the priest who 'marries' the couple, and yet this is not truly the case. The priest may indeed be solemnising what already exists, and may be formally recognising this (on behalf of the state or, together with the gathered assembly, on behalf of the community of faith), but it is difficult to argue that it is at the moment of declaring the couple married that something ontological has occurred. That is not to diminish the importance of the public making of vows, but it is to suggest that they signify something that is already happening within the relationships that is being celebrated.

It is for this reason that the frequent insistence on no sexual intercourse before marriage between those who are engaged is so puzzling (not least given marriage's history). Far too many Christians still treat the moment of the declaration of marriage as the starting gun for sexual intimacy, yet given this intimacy is part of the relationality of the couple and it seems both arbitrary and bizarre to suggest that such intimacy is a special case whereas all other forms of intimacy are already entered into to some degree (as would be hoped for if a couple has made the decision to commit to one another).[6] Here we see both the over-emphasis of the

---

[5]   It is fascinating that covenant *per se* is so clearly recognised as central to the current practice of exclusive opposite sex, opposite gender marriage in the Church of England, for example in the popularity of the use of Ruth 1:16 in such services. That this is a reading about a covenant between two people of the same sex and gender, *and* that this is not a romantic covenant, appears to have been missed by many who make use of this reading and yet continue to oppose same-sex, same-gender marriage based on covenant!
[6]   Sexual intimacy is surely part of the *kairos* moment of marriage as sacramental along with the other creators and manifestations of becoming one flesh.

'specialness' of sex[7] yet also a total lack of recognition that it is part and parcel of relationality and not an addendum to human nature. This is to say nothing of the psychological damage that can be done by placing so much emphasis on the human invention of the 'wedding night', or indeed by separating out the sexual in this way from the rest of the couple's relating.[8]

Before turning to a discussion of complementarity, let us briefly return to the 'creation' in creation ordinance, and ask how this might be understood in the light of our queering the debate. Much has been made of the 'creation' element of marriage in reference to Adam and Eve in the Genesis narrative – where Adam is said to be 'married' to Eve despite the absence of a vowed covenant (and without a clear meaning of the Hebrew text), and where Genesis 2:24 ('therefore a man leaves his father and his mother and clings to his wife, and they become one flesh') has been used as a prescriptive phrase that excludes same-sex, same-gender relationships from marriage. Yet it is beyond the realms of serious theology for us to suggest either that the Genesis story should be taken as historical fact, or that there is a single understanding of 'marriage' in the Bible. We have seen throughout our argument that the 'becoming one flesh' speaks primarily to relationality and the building up of relationship, and if we

---

[7] The February 2023 debate in the General Synod of the Church of England contained some deeply bizarre and thoughtless comments in this regard. Heterosexual speakers spoke about how the blessing of same-sex, same-gender relationships would devalue their own, without any apparent recognition of the offensiveness of their comments. A particularly egregious example was when a speaker explained to the Synod that she had waited for marriage to have sex and the potential that gay people might be having sex outside of marriage was making this harder for her and people like her and mocking her sacrifice. It was remarkable that such an argument was being made by someone opposing the introduction of same-sex marriage – surely a simple answer to her conundrum.

[8] This also appears to do quite significant damage to the understanding of relationship in couples for whom the overtly sexual plays a smaller or less significant part in the overall development of 'one flesh'.

approach this passage as having theological applicability to humankind rather than as a historical narrative that is primarily exclusive, then we surely mine a much richer seam. To appreciate that the Genesis narrative (and Jesus' use of it) opens insights for us into what the church later calls marriage is not in question – but we must surely be willing to see the 'gift of God in creation' as being an invitation to a dynamic and ever deepening engagement with God's creation of humankind and their ontological makeup rather than as a direction to read the creation narratives in a reductive way.

COMPLEMENTARITY

We will not detain ourselves for long in a discussion of the tiresome arguments made by proponents of cis-heteronormativity that suggest that human beings can only be 'complementary' to one another because of their different anatomy. The argument made can be as infantile as a suggestion that complementarity is about penis fitting into vagina, and whilst there may be more nuanced versions, nonetheless these are frequently reduced to conversations about 'essential differences' between men and women which are unevidenced, unconvincing, or outright contested. For the purpose of our argument, and based on even a brief survey of human existence, we are simply dismissing this out of hand – yet some of the wider questions that conversations about perceived complementarity raise remain interesting. We might ask ourselves, for example, whether gender or even sex is theologically purposive – something we have addressed in earlier chapters. We might ask, too, whether what is most theologically important about genuine complementarity of creatures is the differences between people (however we choose to categorise that, rightly or wrongly), or whether the creation stories and human experience really point to the importance of similarity instead.

Mandy Ford draws this tension by making reference to feminist theology:

> There is a paradox arising out of feminist theology (and which is mirrored in other minority theologies): on the one hand, there is a tendency to stress the difference between men and women (or between the dominant party and the 'other'), particularly psychologically, and to argue for the recovery or integration of 'female traits' such as embodied experience, emotional intelligence and so on; on the other, there is a call for equality which downplays the difference between the genders, not only in social and economic roles, but also in the church.[9]

Queer relationships allow us to play with the tension between difference and downplayed difference, because in queer couples (for example) there are likely to be significant differences in a host of areas between the two people, and yet at the same time the traditional categorisation of sex or gender does not apply. Because of this, we are able to ask questions without the inevitable gender and sex power imbalances that wider society imposes on relationships and on marriage specifically (although with an eye to other imbalances which will doubtless remain, implicit and explicit). By doing this, we are able to more fully understand the meaning of the 'one flesh' in a metaphysical way – finding our definition not in a crude description of what fits where, but instead in understanding the oneness primarily in ontological rather than physical terms. To put it another way, that queer couples become one flesh is self-evident – thus we are quite properly drawn to understand the one flesh in this metaphysical way. Patrick Cheng describes this evocatively and beautifully at the very start of *Radical Love*:[10]

[9] Mandy Ford, *God, Gender, Sex and Marriage* p.50
[10] Patrick Cheng, *Radical Love* p.ix

When I met and fell in love with my husband, Michael, almost two decades ago, something radical happened. I experienced the boundaries between myself and the outside world dissolving in a way that I had never experienced before. The boundaries that had separated me from other people in the past – intellectually, emotionally, and physically – became fluid. Michael and I were no longer two separate and distinct persons, but rather two connected human beings with permeable borders.

Cheng goes on to say that his 'standard definitions of who a "man" was allowed to fall in love with ... no longer held true', and 'most importantly, the boundaries between God and me began to dissolve'. This is, surely, the meaning of becoming one flesh – a meaning filled with Biblical and Christian themes, and one in which the male-female divide is simply not necessary. As we have said before, that does not reduce the impact of the male or femaleness, or indeed whatever sexual and gender identity is experienced, on the person who holds that identity in relationship, nor on the relationship itself, but it also helps us to free ourselves from placing our emphasis on the 'man and woman' as our basis for relationship and our willingness to baptise what is far too frequently merely human cultural convention. Here, too, perhaps, we get a vision of what consummation in relationship might truly mean, away from the asinine suggestion that consummation occurs at 'first' sexual intercourse (itself increasingly unlikely to take place on the wedding night!) – consummation as a process of drawing closer to one another and becoming the one flesh that Cheng so movingly speaks of.

LOYALTY AND FIDELITY

Of course, we must recognise that not all covenants remain untouched or unsullied, and adultery is first amongst the ways that such a covenant might be demeaned – although anything but the only way. Indeed, as we have explored the meaning of relationship and the place of sexual intimacy in the building up of this relationship (and the building up of the self alongside this), we can perhaps engage more fully with the metaphysical and ontological assault that sexual infidelity can wreak, whilst at the same time also recognising why a covenant might be demeaned by more than simply sexual infidelity. The long-lasting covenant as an ontological reality is not merely sexual, and indeed the sexual is a physical manifestation and symbol of much else beside. At the centre of such a long-lasting covenant is deep seated commitment, and sacrifice, freely chosen, and it is because of this sacrificial and potentially costly (in some senses) channelling of desire that fidelity spreads much further than the merely sexual. In turn, sexual infidelity (or sexual violence) may speak of or lead to a fissure in the greater edifice, tearing into the loyalty and freely poured out love that sits at the heart of covenantal relationship.

Queerness allows us to decategorise unfaithfulness and instead recognise it as a continuum that includes the sexual and yet which integrates with those other parts of our lives which meet in covenant. It is through having a more holistic understanding of faithfulness (the essence of the vowed nature of covenant) that we are then able to approach relationships with a greater level of both realism but also integrity. Taking a queer approach to long-lasting covenant then allows us to build up and understand such covenants better, and allows the church to have something to say that makes sense of Biblical injunctions against divorce beyond discussions of what is or is not acceptable for someone in a marriage to get up to with someone who is not their spouse (the parallels with the equally inadequate categorical response on the permissibility of sexual intercourse to those in same-sex, same-gender relationships is clear to see).

We might here draw on two examples to illustrate this point. Many (if not all) people in long-lasting covenanted relationships will be tempted to fantasise sexually about those with whom they are not in relationship, either in masturbation or with no overt sexual activity. Of course, some will then go on to act on these fantasies, but for now we are interested more in the fantasies themselves.[11] Given all we have said above, it is doubtless the case that any such fantasy will impact upon the covenantal relationship, although it is likely to be different for different individuals and couples. It may appear somewhat strict to pick up on this point, as it appears that such fantasising is a normal part of human sexual variation and may, indeed, aid in individuals' psychological health. Nonetheless, it does bring to mind Jesus' teaching in Matthew 5, in which he does not pull his punches:

> 'You have heard that it was said, "You shall not commit adultery." But I say to you that everyone who looks at a woman with lust has already committed adultery with her in his heart. If your right eye causes you to sin, tear it out and throw it away; it is better for you to lose one of your members than for your whole body to be thrown into hell. And if your right hand causes you to sin, cut it off and throw it away; it is better for you to lose one of your members than for your whole body to go into hell.'

It is unlikely that many congregations have heard teaching on lust that takes quite this strong a line, and we might indeed think that Jesus is making use of hyperbole in what he has to say! Yet these words do cohere with our queer exploration of sexuality and relationship – that far from acts and desires being easily separable, the links between them remain extremely strong. The impact of inappropriately directed desire on covenantal relationship is therefore something that we must take seriously and the pretence that such desires do not exist does not mean that they will simply go away.

A development of this particular example might be

---

[11] We might think here of our commentary on desire in the preceding chapter.

pornography.[12] There is much to say about the role of pornography in modern life, the role of genuine consent, and the impact on those involved in the industry, for which there is not space here, but we must recognise that in pornography there is a form of objectification of other human persons that is entirely without covenantal basis. Because of this, it is hard to see how its use – most particularly by those within covenantal relationships – can be seen as much different in nature to infidelity, and yet culturally (and perhaps through psychological conditioning, too) we do not afford it this level of seriousness in debate.

It is not the purpose of this chapter to embark on a prudish or unrealistic campaign against particular sexual practices, but it is clear that for pornography in particular, by queering the categories of sexual misdemeanour and the associated threats to covenantal relationship we may indeed find ourselves asking searching questions about the decisions that our society and culture (and church) have made in terms of our priorities for censure and concern. This is not a comfortable process, but we must surely follow the implications of our arguments. Of course, the arguments (and implications of these arguments) around fantasy and pornography are somewhat different for those in and out of long-lasting covenantal relationship, yet we must surely remain wary of sexual intercourse losing the genuineness of the 'intercourse' despite appearances (for this reason, masturbation with pornography is different to masturbation without, for example). Whether we are willing to objectify other human beings for selfish sexual pleasure in which there

---

[12] Or, indeed, sexting or the use of sex chat rooms in which the user interacts with the object of their sexual desire virtually. Such practices appear to be a form of 'no touch' infidelity, and yet it is likely that we consider them to be lesser than having sexual intercourse with a non-spouse. Of course, there is a continuum here too – for example, talk amongst friends which errs into the sexually inappropriate. Our focus on actions has meant that we simply do not take this kind of sexual behaviour seriously, and such behaviours can be excused without serious attention being paid to the meaning of 'exclusive' in sexual covenant.

is no communication or intercourse whatsoever is, perhaps, an issue for the modern world, yet it is surely one that we as Christians should be willing to engage in conversation about.[13]

MARRIAGE AS HISTORICAL REALITY

Before we return to our queer challenge to the idea of marriage itself, it is worth briefly turning to something that has been all-too-often ignored in conversations about marriage. Much ink has been spilt in condemnations of the 'redefinition of marriage' that queer people are supposed to have undertaken in recent years, yet even a brief engagement with the history of the institution would make it abundantly clear that marriage has been redefined, and refined, time after time. The idea that there is a single category of 'Biblical marriage' is ridiculous – whilst it is true that there are no obvious examples of same-sex, same-gender marriage in the Bible, there are also precious few examples of what we would today call marriage either!

This has implications for our reading of scriptural passages on marriage (not least those of St Paul[14] and

---

[13] Interestingly, passively watching pornography is seen as entirely separate from – for example – sitting in a room and passively observing people having sex, even though both activities share almost the entire scenario in common. In many ways, pornography is actually a more problematic form of sexual expression, because whilst watching other people having sex in the same room might not be equivalent to active sexual intercourse, nonetheless there is a level of human personal engagement that is likely to be taking place, even if only before and after the act. It remains fascinating that many married couples will excuse their partner watching pornography, and yet if the other scenario occurred, they would perceive this as cheating. This perhaps highlights the importance of the social-sexual in such encounters.

[14] We might think in particular here of 1 Corinthians 7, and ask whether this is supposed to be an edict for all time or a response to a local (in terms of time and space) example. When reading passages like this, we do well to ask *why* St Paul is saying what he is saying – what is driving his perspective (for example, what does he mean by 'in view of the impending crisis' or 'present necessity', depending on the translation, in verse 26)?

Jesus), as whilst it is tempting to imagine that we can read our own context into the scriptures, this is hardly a safe way to engage theologically. For much of the history of marriage, including marriage sanctioned by the church, women have been seen and treated as property (which perhaps explains Jesus' explanation that marriage will not exist in the age to come), and even a passing understanding of history will remind us of the eugenic, racist, classist and ableist dogmas which have been attached to the institution in the past few hundred years alone.

That marriage has been redefined and saved from much of this abysmal baggage is a cause for rejoicing. Indeed, cis-heterosexuals have themselves redefined marriage in recent times through making it about love rather than family ties, property, or protection! Yet for all this, queerphobia and a commitment to cis-heteronormativity has led to an outright refusal to allow queer people a seat at the marriage feast. It is little more than an absurdity – and a queerphobic one at that.

DOES MARRIAGE EXIST?

Much as we asked in previous chapters about sex and gender, here we might ask ourselves a similar question about marriage – does it actually exist? The Biblical record on this is, perhaps, even clearer than on sex and gender – it appears that Jesus denies the existence of marriage in heaven in Matthew 22:30 (or 'in the resurrection' as the NRSVUE has it), suggesting that even if he recognises marriage on earth – with the caveats as above about what it is that Jesus is recognising[15] – this is a temporary arrangement (a 'pastoral accommodation', as arrangements to permit LGBTQI clergy

---

[15] This point deserves further exploration – perhaps it is because of Jesus' understanding of marriage in the context of His day that He argues that that particular manifestation of marriage will no longer exist.

to exist within the heteronormative paradigm has often been euphemistically called). Thus, what we might ask ourselves is whether marriage as a metaphysical category actually exists, or whether it is either one state amongst many on a continuum, or whether it is categorical, but only before the resurrection.

In many ways, this is a key question for us to engage with as a church that focuses more on relationship than on categories of relationship – do we still need marriage as a discrete entity, and does it mean anything in particular? In other words, is it a discrete sacrament or is it simply one manifestation amongst many of what is really important, which is relationality? Does it actually need to be redeemed?

The church does appear to suggest that marriage is an important human category – a human category given as a 'gift of God in creation', that refers to something discrete. In offering services of blessing, it offers to marriage something that is not offered to other forms of relationship – although we might also ask what is meant by blessing in this context, and what is actually being blessed.[16] The church therefore appears to suggest that the married state is itself discrete and has a particular purpose for individuals. In the words of the queer Episcopalian priest Liz Edman, it is 'a spiritual relationship – a sacred relationship – that is expressed sexually as well as spiritually, physically, emotionally, economically, and so on', which 'is a singular experience that differs in quality and intensity from anything else we humans do'.[17]

Of course, it is entirely possible to get caught in a discussion about semantics rather than about the thing itself, much as churches have that approve of 'civil unions' but cannot bring themselves to refer to these as marriages. However, the point remains as to whether marriage truly is a discrete state (even if the boundaries of marriage with other

[16] Readers may find Andrew Davison's *Blessing* (London: Canterbury Press, 2014) helpful to delve deeper into this.
[17] Elizabeth Edman, *Queer Virtue: What LGBTQ People Know About Life and Love and How It Can Revitalize Christianity* (Boston, MA: Beacon, 2016) p.69

points on the continuum are somewhat fluid, and even if those who are in 'married' relationships would never conceptualise them in this way). Yet we might ask, to help ourselves answer this question, what precisely it is that makes such relationships categorical. It is here that we might find ourselves in deep disagreement, not least because the naming of something as categorically marriage necessarily excludes other forms of relationship from this category. Because of the sacramental nature of marriage, and its particular role in the life of the church, this exclusion (probably) inevitably also leads to a hierarchy of relationship, something that has been seen in the 'equal but different' treatment of Church of England queer clergy who are permitted to enter Civil Partnerships but not marriage. Whether this is a circle that can be squared remains to be seen.

Part of the answer to the question of what distinguishes marriage, if anything – although only part, because of the possibility of this answer also relating to other forms of relationship – is to begin by asking what marriage as a recognised state is for. This is subtly different to asking what covenantal relationships are for, yet it is also not entirely clear that the church must formally recognise something as marriage for it to *be* marriage. What we are asking here is whether there are any characteristics that are necessary for something to be marriage beyond it being covenant – and whether that is a question of gradation or of categorisation. Yet we are also asking about what the relevance of the church *formally recognising* something as marriage might be, too – whether there is anything that such a formal recognition might imbue such a relationship with, and whether the church might rightly have expectations from such a formally recognised (solemnised, for example) state?

This brings us back to conversations about whether there is a single blueprint for successful long-lasting covenantal relationship, and whether – if there is not – there is nonetheless a preferred blueprint with certain characteristics that the church might bless particularly. Should marriage, for example, have a requirement for permanence? What role does mutual fulfilment and staying in the relationship for the benefit of the other hold? To what degree should marriage hold an expectation of exclusivity – for example, should marriages be closed to the possibility of consensual extra-marital sexual intercourse (whether by each partner separately, or together)? Should polyamorous relationships be excluded from marriage? Most importantly, how do we justify our categorising in this way? Is 'is this marriage' really the question we should be asking?

We shall return to some of these questions in our final chapter. For now, however, we might simply suggest that engaging with them is central to our being able to put forward a coherent, convincing, and sufficient argument in a world that still believes our only contribution is to say 'marriage is between a man and a woman', and expect that this will end the debate. As a church, we are not called to merely replace one form of categorisation with another – instead, we must do our homework to determine why we believe what we do, in the process finding theological justification that will stand up to serious scrutiny. Our church is in desperate need of revival and restoration – and queerness offers us the tools to embark on this mission. Let us turn now to how this queerness can stimulate revitalisation in more than merely the battleground sacrament of marriage.

9

REORIENTING THE CHURCH

It goes without saying that much of what needs to be said about queer people in the life of the church will relate to those very things we have touched on in the last few chapters – sex, relationship, marriage. We must not be naïve, of course, and imagine that the insights that queer theology can give us in these areas are only applicable to queer people. Yet we must also not fall into the trap of imagining that there is a neatly circumscribed area of the church's to which queer theology and queer lives and loves might contribute, and that beyond this we can go on our merry way and cede the ground to cis-heteronormativity. To do so is to fundamentally lose sight of the importance of the queering of our common life. Queering is an all-encompassing project, one that seeks to free all the parts of our life in community and in communion from the unreality in which it so often finds itself trapped, and thus has implications for much of who we are, what we say, and what we do as a church.

This project is challenging because the church – including the Church of England – is itself an agent of normativity. Those who have sought to challenge this positionality throughout Christian history have been routinely silenced and expelled from the common life of the church, described as unorthodox or heretical, and at times faced extraordinary levels of persecution and even violence in the name of 'the church', which should be more correctly described as 'in the name of normativity'. This is true both of the church as an institution, in that its processes, its hierarchy, its own institutions, and so on, all tend towards a culture of normativity, and also of the church as a perceived entity. These two build one another up, and hence perception can further cement institutionalised normativity – those in the church feel the need to perform in a particular way because of how they are perceived by society, and conversely society grows to expect church leaders to act, look, and think a particular way.

This perception of the church as an agent of normativity leads to its being viewed as a tool of conservatism and of social propriety. Much of the cultural baggage of 'respectability' that the church has picked up has little to do with its historical place in society (we might think of the church before Constantine) or indeed its theology, and yet for those who wish to retain the church as such an agent, careful and selective reading of scripture can easily be used to suggest that 'respectability' is of the essence of the church itself. As the symbols of the faith, such as the cross, become so culturally normative in and of themselves, it is hard for those within and without the church to recognise the sheer offensiveness and unrespectable nature of so much of the Christian heritage. Of course, as salt loses its saltiness, it is unsurprising that the church appears to have so little to say to the modern world.[1]

There have always been those who have sought to stir up the radical potential of the church, although as we have mentioned they have frequently been side-lined, ostracised, or worse. The contemporary opposition to those who are now seen as such radicals (for example Francis of Assisi, and perhaps to a lesser degree even Pope Francis) is frequently brushed over in later accounts, and indeed even those who

---

[1]   One wonders whether the Synodal Way might be an opportunity for the Roman Catholic Church to rediscover its own saltiness.

are later recognised as the great figures of faith that they are, are often domesticated and have their radical edge removed in church re-tellings of their stories in order for them to found 'appropriate' to include in the traditions of the church.

Frequently these radicals have been painted by the disciples of normativity as those who have lost their moorings and who are dangerously trying to subvert the church and the work of the Holy Spirit. In hindsight, however, they are infrequently seen in such a way, instead being recognised as those who are instead calling the church to a refinement of its life and purpose, through a shedding of the cultural baggage that it has far too frequently baptised. In recent years, we might think of Liberation Theologians as being such radicals – initially rejected by those who, in some ways understandably, felt it necessary to protect the church from instability and change. Queer theologians, too, sit in this stream, and it is without doubt that the church of the future will recognise this. For now, however, the powers of normativity remain strong and the voices of the marginal are further marginalised by those in power – a stifling of the Holy Spirit.

RADICAL SILENCE

We might reflect for a moment as to why this might be. It is certainly the case that those who have power in any institution are unlikely to want to lose it, and that is sadly also true of an institution that is built on *kenosis* and on the giving up of power.[2] We shall turn to questions of conservation, and the importance of challenge in the life of the church, below – for now we might also recognise the lack of courage that

---

[2] It is for this reason that Philippians 2 might serve as a better 'mission statement' for the church than the increasingly banal diocesan mottos in the Church of England. A particularly poorly thought out one is that of Southwell and Nottingham, which has inexplicably chosen the phrase 'Wider Younger Deeper' as its tagline – ill-advised even by the standards of the wider Church of England.

appears to blight far too many of our leaders in the modern age.[3] Our bishops, in particular, appear to be people chosen because they can 'keep the show on the road' rather than because they have a helpfully disruptive vision – and those who are lauded as being disruptors seem to actually move the church closer to worldly culture than away from it (for example in condemning the mysterious or the sublime in worship), failing to recognise that it is the theological assumptions and misplaced faith in normativity that truly need to be challenged.

This lack of courage is coupled with a refusal to name the obvious, with a preference in the Church of England in particular to do deals behind closed doors and in so doing to shore up the *status quo*. In recent debates about the introduction of prayers and blessings for same-sex, same-gender couples, far too little has been said about the role of money in decision making.[4] Dioceses are being threatened with withdrawal of money by prime agents of normativity, who see their power and hold over decision-making in the church fading away, and yet bishops and others appear desperate to avoid these threats being handled in public, presumably for fear of (yet another) scandal and loss of trust. The reality, of course, is that were such threats made more widely known, then those issuing them might be better judged on their actions and their motivations, and because of this the potency of their ability to coerce the church might be reduced.

The outright refusal of those opposed to change to accept any compromise whatsoever is frequently described by them as being a theological imperative, yet as we have

---

[3] Of course, there may be, in the mix, some genuine fear of loss of the richness of the Christian tradition, but blunt and unthinking conservatism does not help this cause.

[4] For example, one fringe group, the Church of England Evangelical Council, has suggested euphemistically that 'wide scale and far reaching action would need to be taken by those opposed to such prayers': https://ceec. info/ceec-formally-responds-to-house-of-bishops-proposals-and-subsequent-public-communications/ [accessed October 7th 2023].

seen through these pages it is far closer to an ideological imperative. If the church was more willing to engage with a full-scale assault on cis-heteronormativity, involving a radical reorientation to the core of Christianity and its theological truths, then this would become plain to see – and the church should be willing to do so, because cis-heteronormativity is not theology but ideology. It may be that after purifying the doctrine of the church from cis-heteronormative ideology – as much as is possible – then theological opposition to same-sex, same-gender marriage might remain, and if this were the case then we could truly debate it on theological rather than ideological terms. To date, we remain in the realm of ideology.

Throughout history, sex has been used as an agent of power, and whilst the current manifestation of this power dynamic might be more subtle, nonetheless it is notable that sex remains at the centre of these conversations – conversations that frequently revolve around the male penetrative act. It is beyond the scope of this book to reflect on this in any great detail, but it is notable that so much time and effort has been poured out by those opposing change in churches looking towards change in a pursuit of discipline around sex and sexuality. Not only is the conversation usually ideological and not theological, but very little time is spent discussing the underlying relationship of sex to human anthropology, and much more is spent trying to ensure that rules and regulations are in place to control other people's – most particularly queer people's – sex lives.[5]

This brings us back to the fact raised earlier in this book, that whilst queer people have been expected not to have sex because it is 'non-procreative', non-queer people

[5] In a recent Church of England meeting to determine the place of rightly ordered sexuality in queer lives at which the author was present, a leading opponent of change – themselves a bishop – stated 'I am actually very interested in the sex lives of my clergy – there need to be strong rules here'. This was a rather inadvertent admission of the fact that within ecclesial dialogue, even amongst the bishops (and hence teachers of the faith), control and discipline (for which read punishment) have trumped the deeper questions we are trying to explore in this book.

have been free to engage in all kinds of sex acts that are objectively non-reproductive without so much as a question being raised. Unfortunately, this is entirely consistent with the way that sex has been managed by the church through the millennia – we might think of the sexual infidelity of popes, kings, bishops, and priests, in some cases up until the current day. Yet similarly, whilst the institution *qua* institution has been an agent of normativity, it is also the case that those within it – including those holding power – have frequently acted in ways that is anything but normative.

CELIBACY AND FRIENDSHIP

This, of course, ranges from the hypocritical to the entirely open. Sexually unfaithful popes might sit at one end of this continuum, together with queer-bashing televangelists who are secretly bedding their male lovers, or, indeed, bishops who oppose (or who cowardly refuse to argue for) same-sex, same-gender marriage whilst having queer sexual encounters themselves. Yet one group that we have not yet spoken in detail about are those who practice celibacy as a religious vow. Such an existence in a church-manufactured world of cis-heteronormative, nuclear-family-adoring ideology is totally left field – so much so as to be considered, perhaps, queer. Yet before we emphasise the potentially radical nature of such a way of life, we ought to interrogate it a little further.

Celibacy does not come in a single flavour. Indeed, for many it is not a 'call' but a demand and a condition (albeit one unequally policed) – thinking most particularly here of Roman Catholic priests, but also queer priests who willingly (a contested term) abide by the Church of England's requirement that they remain celibate. There is much to be said about celibacy itself for which there is little space here,[6] but for now we ought to recognise that abstinence

---

[6] This is dealt with in some detail in *Queer Holiness*.

from sexual acts may be the lay understanding of celibacy yet fails to take into account the psychological and indeed ontological questions that are raised. We might ask ourselves what exactly is being abstained from – and for what purpose? Is it merely the sexual act, and if so, does this mean that the sexual-social might be built up for another but not brought to completion? If so, why? In addition, if this is a demand rather than an internal calling, then how might this be defended by the institution that makes such a demand? We might talk of theological themes such as sacrifice and desire for God, but given what we now know about human psychological make-up, it is by no means clear that this is a closed theological question. Given the abuse scandals in the church, it is not only open but urgent.

That is not to say that there is no such thing as chosen celibacy – however we might define that – and for some people it may indeed be a particular calling which does indeed include sacrifice but which also brings with it great spiritual reward. The issue with celibacy more generally is that it remains so uncritically practised and demanded, and because of this the questions that need to be asked in order to test its fidelity to the Christian tradition and to Christian anthropology remain largely unasked, let alone unanswered. We might mention here, too, the importance of the church grappling with questions of singleness – chosen or otherwise. Singleness, indeed, requires further definition in terms of the avoidance of long-lasting covenanted-ness whilst possibly being open to casual sex, and also the emphasis placed on friendship in any such discussions.[7]

We have briefly touched on friendship previously, but it is

---

[7] The Church of England has included prayers for Covenanted Friendships in their 'Prayers and Love and Faith', which unhelpfully muddies the waters between friendship and exclusive covenant and appears to be an attempt to placate an imaginary constituency who seek such a thing. It is not at all clear what a covenanted friendship is – unless the Church of England can clearly state what Covenanted Friendships are, it really should not be providing prayers for them.

worth drawing attention here to the woeful lack of emphasis that the church places on friendship, and in particular Christian companionship – friendship which is often found between those who would not form such a bond if they did not have involvement in a local or wider Christian community. Once again, there is not the space here to fully engage with this issue, but much of what has been discussed in our conversations about relationality and covenant is surely relevant, as – perhaps – is our discussions of casual sex. Whilst it is clear that many people tend towards some form of exclusive (however this might be defined) and permanent (at least in aspiration) relationship with one other person, this is by no means the case across the board, and the church ought to be more alert to and cognisant of this.

It is arguable, indeed, that our first workings out of relationship should be in the context of friendship, and that this should be the basis upon which we do our thinking on exclusive relationships. Whether there is something distinctive in nature rather than merely degree in the development of romantic, exclusive relationships beyond friendship is something that requires further reflection, not least because it has something to say about our purpose and our ontology as human beings. However, what is abundantly clear is that we do an injustice to those who do not seek or do not find romantic relationships if our entire Christian story appears tended towards them, implicitly suggesting that it is only through these that human beings can be fulfilled. We do an injustice, too, to the doctrine of the incarnation and to the fully human nature of Jesus Christ if we suggest that a romantic relationship is the pinnacle of theological hope.

A focus on marriage (and the family) is partly to blame, and this is particularly the case since 'Christian' marriage has been restricted to non-queer people, meaning that much of the noise in recent years has been about extending this normative institution to queer people rather than questioning the institution's overly central role in Christianity's officially expressed narrative. The work of queering will not, in other words, be done if we simply replace heterosexual marriage with a different form of marriage as the be all and end all of human relating. We can and must do better than this as a church, not least because if we do not, then we remain in unreal discourse and by virtue of this, speak less of God.

A 'COUNTERCULTURAL' CHURCH

As we discussed in Chapter 2, one of the most pernicious and bizarre narratives that has been pushed by those who wish to continue the hegemony of the cis-heteronormative in the church is that by listening to the voices of queer people, the church is somehow bending to culture and losing its 'countercultural' nature. It is high time for those in power in the church to pay attention to the true dynamics of cultural engagement that the church is employed in – and called to. It is without doubt that our promotion of cis-heteronormativity is in no small way associated with the church's endless longing for respectability that we discussed at the start of this chapter. This longing can mean that we are willing to overlook those things which we might otherwise interrogate, and call some things theological when they are more correctly theologically justified cultural phenomena.

One example of this might be the endless arguments around women's ordination. In Chapter 3, we considered this from the standpoint of what sex and gender really mean, but here we might also consider it in the light of cultural influences. To what extent are our 'theological' arguments – on both sides of this debate – grounded in theology rather than in cultural norms and stereotypes? Similarly to our acceptance or otherwise of queer people as integrated, social-sexual wholes, to what degree can we truly extricate ourselves from our cultural milieu? How can we be sure that what we are calling Christian is not merely culturally Christian?

This is particularly difficult for churches, like the Church of England, that themselves come from a place of social privilege. The Church of England's perspective on marriage matters because it forms part of the state apparatus, and its ministers are state registrars in the context of marriage. It is by no means clear that we can neatly separate the cultural from the theological in such a setting. The risk, then, is that patriarchal and cis-heteronormative culture, which itself may have been influenced by and been an influence on particular expressions of Christianity, is able to seep so deep into a church's self-understanding that the church loses sight of its fundamental nature. For the Church of England, there is a British exceptionalism that also feeds into the church's self-understanding, impacting on its relationship with the Anglican Communion and with other denominations. An uncritical performance of the role of Established Church runs the risk of the church itself becoming a willing participant in oppression and silencing which – if it were better interrogated – goes against its fundamental ecclesial identity. Normativity is the glue which holds together this dangerous edifice, and as we shall see, allowing it to break apart would produce a far healthier and more authentic church than if we continue to focus on keeping a creaking ship afloat.

CAN ANYTHING GOOD COME OUT OF NAZARETH?

All this being said, it is nonetheless the contention of this book that the church matters, and it is because it matters that we need to take these issues and challenges seriously. The church is called to be the Body of Christ on Earth, and when it fails to be so, it fails to fulfil the mission which it was given, and fails to be in true continuity with the church founded by Jesus Christ. A church that looks to exclude based on arbitrary human categories is not one that is able to participate in the creative will and action of God.

We spoke in Part 1 about the queasiness that we might rightly feel about the idea of 'inclusion'. Much worthy talk is made of 'including' different groups into the church, yet there are two fundamental errors at the heart of such thinking. The first we have touched on – it is not for us to do the including, but for God – the Eucharistic table being a key example of this being played out in practice, where invitations need not be mediated by anyone but by God Godself. Some conservative Christians are known to refuse to 'receive communion' alongside queer people (particularly those known to be in romantic relationships, 'sexually active' or otherwise), basing this on the recommendation in 1 Corinthians 5 not to 'even eat with' someone who is 'sexually immoral'. Not only does such a refusal suggest that the term 'sexually immoral' is entirely clear, and indeed that Paul's prohibitions here are for all time rather than culturally or contextually dependent, but it also belies a fundamental misunderstanding about what is happening in communion. The Eucharist is primarily a metaphysical event – a sacrament that through physical things opens the efficacious window into the life and work of the Holy Spirit. Indeed, when we commune we do so not only with those at the altar rail next to us, but with Christians throughout the world – and, indeed, with Christians throughout time and space. To 'refuse to take communion alongside' is to fail to recognise the essence and meaning of the Eucharistic meal – it is to attempt to define it in human categories, and in so doing, to weaponise it and usurp what is rightly God's.

'The owner of the Eucharist is the one who supposedly is presiding over it since its first celebration in the Upper Room ... and he is always inviting his friends to share his meal with him in joy and love', says Jaci Maraschin, and it is an 'unbelievable and ugly atrocity' when 'a particular segment of the so-called Christian Church took possession of something that does not belong to it, retaining it to its particular historical group'.[8] Whilst Maraschin is speaking

---

[8]   Jaci Maraschin, 'Worship and the Excluded' in Marcella Althaus-Reid, ed., Liberation Theology and Sexuality (Aldershot: Ashgate, 2006) pp.163-78, p.172

here about 'the stone in the midst of the pathway' in ecumenical refusals to share at the Eucharistic table, his words could just as easily refer to those who choose to act as host in the presence of the true Host, and prevent or object to queer people fully entering into the Eucharistic feast. There is much more to be said about this, but for now we must surely recognise the futility of placing human exclusion above God's inclusion.

The second reason that speaking of inclusion is wrong, is because in doing so we fail to recognise the real scandal at the heart of the Christian faith, which is not that queer people are included, but that anybody is! In all our extraordinary human reality, in our failings, and in our glories, in our successes and in our failures, however good or bad or indifferent or right or wrong we might be – all of this was loved into being and all of this is loved into redemption. God's love for each single thread of our lives, each fibre of our being, is so infinite and so extraordinary that Jesus died for us. And God's love for us is for us in our whole humanity – because of our humanity, not despite it. Queer people offer the church the opportunity to see this, if only she would look.

Yet when we look at the way that the church includes (or rather, excludes) and how the world beyond does, we are too frequently met with a picture that is topsy turvy – where the world's willingness to see the real in the queer is more pronounced than the church's. It is beyond doubt that despite recent gentle moves towards a recognition of queer holiness, the Church of England's culture remains deeply unhealthy for and towards queer people, lay and ordained alike. An acceptance of queer people into marriage is not going to change that (and is not currently even on the cards) – instead, the work needs to be done from first principles. Yet it is also true that whilst queer people may suffer from this disproportionately, nonetheless the culture negatively impacts on others, too. We might think particularly of the inextricable link between cis-heteronormativity and patriarchy, for example, and the way that queer people and women are all too frequently subject to the whims of cis-heterosexual men. Yet we might go further, considering the impact of this culture on other marginalised people, for example, Black people, disabled people – and in doing so, recognise that the cis-heteronormative contains within it not only damaging sex and gender normativity.

The challenge for the church is that its starting point needs to be that we – that is, queer people, and people more generally outside a particular hegemonic mould – exist, that our lives are holy, and, to coin a phrase, the church needs to get over it. It needs to do so because there is something essential in listening to the voices of the marginal in truly becoming the whole that we are called to be. As Liz Edman puts it, 'I want to encourage people who claim the mantle of Christianity to hone our ability to receive and embrace [the perspectives of queer identity, including the marginalised and the abused] as essential to the vivification of our tradition'.[9] If we are unwilling to listen to them, then we will miss something of the reality of the Kingdom of God, and fail to learn as much about God and the experience of God's people as we might otherwise do. Yet the church, much like Nathanael, far too often asks 'can anything good come out of Nazareth?', rather than taking Philip's advice – 'come and see' (John 1:46). If we can't move beyond asking if queers might have anything to offer, then no wonder we won't listen to them when they do.

THE DISCERNMENT OF LOVE

The problem with recognising that the unlikely might have something to contribute is that we need to begin on a journey of discernment, and such a journey can be rather uncomfortable if we are used to having simplistic categories and easily derivable juridical answers. In

9   Elizabeth Edman, *Queer Virtue* p.5

recognising the holiness of queer people and their loves, we then have to do the hard work of interrogating and refining what we mean when we talk about love. We might find reflections of particular Christian truths in the lives of queer people and their communities,[10] and similarly we might find that an openness to queer relationality also opens our minds to richer understandings of scriptural material.

For example, during debates in the Church of England on new liturgies to pray for and bless same-sex, same-gender couples, there was much disquiet expressed by self-professed conservatives that the Song of Songs might be included as a possible reading in such services because of its allusions to sex. There is not space here to do justice to the reception of this text's genre by different groups in Christian history, but it is worth noting that whether or not a text was recommended for use in such services, given it is a Biblical text it can be used anyway![11] To refuse to even countenance a queer reading of the Song of Songs is to condemn oneself to a cis-heteronormative reading in which the dynamics expressed remain trapped in one particular understanding of human relating (of course, it is particularly interesting to read the Song of Songs as a lesbian poem, in which mutuality of experience rather than hierarchical dynamics might come to the fore). To entirely reject the reality of queer embodiment and its impact on scriptural understanding is to lose a valuable insight into the reality of human life and the reality of God.

---

[10]   Patrick Cheng makes reference to the work of Daniel Helminiak, who suggests that 'the Trinity is reflected in the external life of the LGBT community' through 'friendships beyond gender limitations, equality in relationship, personal growth, and preservation of personal uniqueness'. Daniel Helminiak, *Sex and the Sacred: Gay Identity and Spiritual Growth* (Binghampton, NY: Harrington Park, 2006) pp. 132-36 quoted in Patrick Cheng *Radical Love* p.59

[11]   In many ways this was just another example of the tiresome rear-guard action to try to prevent a Synodically agreed change coming into play, somewhat scandalously headed by a number of bishops.

FROM THE INSTITUTIONAL TO THE PERSONAL

Much of what we have said so far relates primarily to the institutional church, and yet we cannot simply pretend that the institutional and the personal are not entwined and impacted upon by the other. An openness to the queer in our institutions also requires us to have an openness to the queer in our own lives – a willingness to have our daily lives, our priorities, and our relationships challenged and changed through this openness. For some of us who are queer, this may prove easier, although because of the fundamentally untrue yet oft repeated suggestion that queer holiness is impossible, we will still find ourselves up against our own implicit biases, queerphobia and cis-heteronormative programming.

Yet we are called not only to say but to believe – and thus to live the reality that restores the rightful place of queer people as citizens of the Kingdom of God, and the rightful place of queering in holding our institutions and our lives to account. It is in magnifying the existence of queer people in the church that we might allow the church to renew itself, and in that process to bring ourselves closer to the Kingdom of God through what the gifts of queering and queerness can offer – gifts of the Holy Spirit. Because queer people are in Christ Jesus, the words of St Paul apply to us just as much to anyone else: 'therefore there is no condemnation for those who are in Christ Jesus' (Romans 8:1). All of us in the church are called to make these words a reality more than a mere aspiration – and it is by refining ourselves and our institutions that we might more truly become the Body of Christ.

10

EMBRACING THE REAL

S o far, we have made what remains in many ways an abstract argument for changing the way we do things as a church. Queering can sometimes feel one step removed from the church on the ground – the way we do things week by week. Yet as Christians, we are called in our own lives and in our corporate life to live out what we believe. This matters in how we engage with one another, in how we do theology, but also in how we enact and respond to the worship and ministry of the church. Queerness reminds us that being serious about reality matters, and what we do as a church needs to bear witness to this reality. We now turn to considering the sacraments, as real expressions of grace, and ask what queerness may have to tell us about their true nature and the grace they might bring.

THE SACRAMENTS AS 'REAL GRACE'

There is not the space here to engage with even the lightest touch with the arguments on the number of sacraments that Anglicans should accept, and instead we will simply work from the assumption that the seven commonly known sacraments – baptism, Eucharist, confirmation, reconciliation, anointing of the sick, marriage and holy orders – all have something of the efficacious window we spoke of in previous chapters to them. Our task, then, is to ask to what degree these sacraments are indeed such efficacious windows to the church and the world in the light of queerness – and to what degree the efficacious beauty of these sacraments is being reduced by being placed in the cis-heteronormative straight-jacket. Similarly, we might ask to what degree these sacraments in and of themselves display queerness, and what a queer lens might be able to enable us to see more clearly when gazing upon them.

We will start by considering the sacrament of initiation, baptism. The Church of England describes it as follows:[1]

> Here we are washed by the Holy Spirit and made clean.
> Here we are clothed with Christ,
> dying to sin that we may live his risen life.
> As children of God, we have a new dignity
> and God calls us to fullness of life.

In baptism, then, we are reclothed with the *Imago Dei*, given an indelible mark of the Holy Spirit, and raised to holiness in Christ. Baptism is 'the beginning of a journey with God that continues for the rest of our lives, the first step in response to God's love'. Because of this, baptism cannot be seen as anything but a total immersion in God's grace and love – the whole person who is being baptised being taken up and clothed in the garments of grace. The 'new dignity' and 'fullness of life' is God's gift to all the baptised, and therefore all those entering into the life of Christ through this sacrament are gifted these things in the same way. God therefore gives dignity and fullness of life through the queerness of the queer – at baptism, we are not disintegrated into different parts, some of which are cut away, but rather our entire social-psychological-sexual-physical selves are wrapped in the holiness that

---

[1] The Church of England, *Baptism and Confirmation*, available here: https://www.churchofengland.org/prayer-and-worship/worship-texts-and-resources/common-worship/christian-initiation/baptism-and [accessed October 7th 2023].

drenches us in the waters of baptism and in this drenching are sanctified.

Of course, we know that baptism is not a magic process, and nor do we immediately stop sinning upon rising from the waters. Yet nonetheless what we can say about baptism is that it imbues our entire selves with grace and dignity, a dignity that is grounded in the holiness of the *Imago Dei* that we are called to carry. Queer people are created and renewed in the very same image and likeness of God as others, and hence our identity is first and foremost found in God in the same way as non-queers.

This focus on identity has been wilfully misrepresented by those who oppose queer equality, by suggesting that queer people put too much emphasis on their queer identity and hence reject their identity in Christ. Nothing could be further from the truth – queer people, however, recognise that the cis-heterosexual is not the only God-given identity (or indeed one at all), and instead hold that their queer identity is part and parcel of their identity in Christ. As Elizabeth Stuart puts it, 'in Christ maleness and femaleness and gay and straight are categories that dissolve before the throne of grace where only the garment of baptism remains'.[2]

This is not the same as suggesting that such categories are not humanly impactful, but rather that they are *unreal* (as we have described previously) in the ultimate reckoning. Because of this, the ultimate orientation in baptism is towards 'the garment of baptism', and hence the ultimate identity for human beings is this garment and all it signifies. Other identities, however real or unreal, are collected up in this garment, but this garment is worn just as much by queer people as by non-queers. Patrick Cheng suggests that Stuart's argument concludes that because of the "inadequacy of all other forms of identity", 'none of the various identities that

---

[2] Elizabeth Stuart, 'Sacramental Flesh' in Gerard Loughlin, ed., *Queer Theology: Rethinking the Western Body* (Oxford: Blackwell, 2007) pp.65-75, 73

lead to church-sanctioned exclusion (for example gender or sexuality) matter',[3] but it is not clear what the directionality of this 'mattering' is. For the individuals concerned, these other identities do matter – and indeed matter because they are helpful descriptors of and for the individual in question. However, their 'not mattering' is really a comment on their not materially impacting the validity or totality of the primary identity in baptism.

This is a tension that queer people (and others whose identity is somewhat forced upon them *in relation to* a normative identity) are used to experiencing. Such a tension is heightened when considering trans people and the expressed discomfort about baptism in a previous identity. Here, the church needs to learn to listen – whether to requests for a form of sacramental renaming and adoption of one's new (or true) identity into the garment of baptism.[4] Effective responses are likely to place the pastoral before the legalistic – yet to do so is not to ignore the sacramentality of the action but rather to find ways for the church to visibly afford trans people the dignity that baptism has *already* afforded them *as them.* The sacramentality of baptism is not at stake – rather, it is necessary for the church to find a way of most effectively holding the tension of identities that all humans experience and value, within the garment of baptism. This is real grace – where sacramentality is seen to engage the whole person and not merely the sum of its (deemed acceptable) parts.

The implications of this taking up of all identities into baptism is seen when we then consider the Eucharist. As we have said, the Eucharistic table is set by God for God's people, and not the other way around, and therefore all the baptised are called to the table. Yet there is more to say than this – for the Body of Christ gathered to receive includes the queer, and if they are excluded then the Body of Christ is

[3] Patrick Cheng, *Radical Love* p.121
[4] Here there is a need for the ritualistic and sacramental which embodies an acknowledgement of something that was included in the garment at the moment of baptism but was not yet known to them or the wider church.

incomplete. Not only this, but the taking up of queer identities into the garment of baptism means that these very queer identities are found in the Body of Christ itself, not only in its manifestation in the church but in its manifestation on the altar.

That we can see the queering of boundaries in baptism and the Eucharist is clear – whether those be the boundaries between heaven and earth, life and death, divine and human, secular and sacred. In the Eucharist, all that have been initiated in baptism are raised to participation in the Body of Christ, and that body is manifested in a queer way itself – both as human (in the church) and divine (in the host). The Eucharist, then, is the ultimate example of the futility of human categorisation – as endless arguments about the nature of the mystery suggest (whether memorialism, transubstantiation, and so on).

Queerness gives us the tools to approach the altar without this need to categorise or prescribe – it allows us to enter the presence of God and experience it, stand in awe of it, and offer worship. Here we bring our whole selves into communion with one another and with God, and here we are fed with that which transgresses all our boundaries. Here our human embodiment meets heavenly embodiment and is reinterpreted in the light of it, the diversity of our humanity reflecting something of the mystery of God and the mystery of the Incarnation. Here, then, we have a foretaste of the queerness of eternity.

We see this obliteration of simplistic categorisation across the other sacraments of the church. In reconciliation, the 'boundaries between guilt and innocence'[5] are queered through forgiveness. In ordination, power and authority are queered in the name of service and humility – and, indeed, the priesthood of all believers itself queers the idea of the professionally religious, imbuing ordination with a directionality that is first towards the people of God in order to

---

[5]   Patrick Cheng, *Radical Love* p.124

build up their priesthood. In anointing we see the boundaries of bodily health and our social-psychological-sexual selves being blurred. In confirmation, we come to the altar and give our assent, and yet we do so not because we choose but because we have been chosen.

Indeed, even the sacraments – whilst descriptively categorised – themselves sit on a continuum of grace. When we meet the sacraments in this way, we enrich their meaning rather than debase them – and indeed we gain an insight into the *real* towards which they point. The sacraments, then, viewed through a queer lens, become windows into eschatological reality – yet they cannot merely remain as windows, but must effect change in us through grace.

QUEER MISSION

We find, then, that those very things that have been captured within a cis-heteronormative church are themselves dressed in the vestments of queerness, if only we had the willingness and the courage to see – and to live out the implications of such a reality. Yet if we are to do this, we need not only to enjoy the weird and the mysterious, the intellectual and abstract reality, but embody this in our practice. As a church, we are called to place a greater emphasis once again on our sacramental life, but to do so not in order to create yet more lists of rules and regulations to determine who is in and who is out, but to offer the sacraments freely and to help those who approach to fully understand the life-giving grace that is poured out in and through them. Our mission then, too, must be imbued with the lessons that this queerness imparts – and we must learn to live in the grey area rather than desperately strive for certainty, focusing on pastoring rather than pronouncing, and getting alongside rather than talking down to. Here, then, we see what participation in the creative will and action of God truly looks like.

For too long, the church has appeared entirely hostile to

queer people, by presenting itself as a bastion of respectability and normativity, and in many cases plainly telling queer people that there is no room at the inn. Queer people have been banned from the sacramental life of the church,[6] and told that they must submit to cis-heteronormative rules of life if they wish to gain access to the Lord who came 'that they may have life and have it abundantly' (John 10:10). The church's utter inability to speak in terms of human flourishing, and instead its determination to begin from a categorical standpoint, has led not only to the collapse of our credibility (moral or otherwise) amongst queer people but amongst many in wider society who see us not only as irrelevant and intellectually moribund, but as agents of evil. Our refusal to engage with scientific evidence about 'conversion therapy', and our refusal to listen to queer people more generally, has led us to a place where it is small wonder that so few people want to have anything to do with us.

At its very heart, the Christian faith and its worldview is properly queer. Despite the protestations of the ideologues, Christianity is a religion that should refuse to bow to human categories and which finds its purpose and calling in the God of mystery, fully human and fully divine. Our Gospel – good news – is for 'all people' and not merely the select few. Our mission will ultimately fail when we see human beings as 'the other', and our engagements with wider culture and society will never prove fruitful when we pretend that 'the world' and 'the church' are discrete categories. It is only by orienting ourselves to God – that is, by facing all that is and looking for the things of God in it – that we will truly be able to live out the Good News.

Yet queering as a methodology, and queer people as those with queer lived experience, can both offer us

---

[6] A particularly egregious example is available here https://www.nbcnews.com/nbc-out/out-news/catholic-diocese-says-gay-trans-people-cant-baptized-receive-communion-rcna8217# [accessed October 7th 2023].

insights into new ways of going about the mission of the church. Mission, of course, is not something that we do but something that we participate in – much like creation (mission being an agent of the new creation). We do not convert people – the Holy Spirit does – and we are merely the Spirit's willing collaborators, vessels of grace. Whilst it is tempting for us to go out and 'tell everybody about Jesus', we may end up doing more good by asking what they know about Him already, what they know about God, or indeed just what they know about love, and fidelity, and goodness, and holiness. Queer people may have much to teach the church about godly living, if we were but willing to listen to them – not least because of their life experiences which all too often include marginalisation, rejection, opposition, and hatred. It is amongst such as these that Jesus went, eating and drinking, walking alongside and loving. That is not a bad place from which to start.

Yet before we turn to this aspect of our mission, we must surely also recognise the insight that queerness can bring to our preconceptions of the church and the world as discrete categories. By queering those categories, we might be more able to see the work of the Holy Spirit within and without the church, working in the lives of those we would least (in our dominant, prejudicial narrative) expect to find the Spirit. We have already seen the woeful misrepresentation of the word 'countercultural' in our ecclesial dialogues, and hence as those called to mission we must surely learn, too, to seek for the essence of what is of God and what is not rather than rely on superficial categorisation with its simplistically coded tokens of meaning. Queerness ultimately calls us to conversation and dialogue – genuine dialogue that helps both parties refine and better understand what God is telling us, through scripture, tradition, reason, experience and the work of the Spirit in the world and in the church. In other words, we might not have all the answers when we go to meet those who have been ostracised by the church – but they may have some of the answers for us.

THE CHRIST OF THE PERIPHERY

As we have said, in Christ's earthly life he spent time amongst precisely those who a 'respectable' church might try to avoid or wish to think weren't on God's radar. God's heart for the poor and marginalised is a consistent narrative of scripture, and yet too often the church has placed itself on the side of the oppressor and not the oppressed in the name of 'stability' or 'orthodoxy'. Our worship of God surely rings hollow in the ears of God if it does not spill out into our lives – for how can we worship God when God's beloved are trampled underfoot?

There is a certain solidarity in marginalisation, which is certainly true amongst queer people. Liz Edman refers to it as follows:[7]

> Now, if you are queer, too, you might take that opportunity to tell me so. And we would both get that fabulous little charge that queer people get recognizing and being recognized by each other, that small but significant feeling of the home that we become for each other just by being ourselves together.

She then goes on to make explicit the link between this kind of solidarity and Christian solidarity:

> This sense of home is a feeling that Christians have known during times when followers of Jesus have been persecuted. The fish symbol was used to identify Christians to each other in the early days of the Roman Empire in much the same way that the lambda became a discreet symbol for queers in the mid-twentieth century.

Queer community – as marginalised community – therefore has much in common with early Christian communities,

---

[7] Elizabeth Edman, *Queer Virtue* p.7

and as such may indeed have much to teach about how Christians might regain some of the solidarity that was needed before the development of post-Constantinian cultural and hegemonic Christianity. Patrick Cheng describes this queer solidarity as 'communities of radical love ... "families" and "bodies" that cut across traditional boundaries that separate us. Indeed, the rainbow flag and annual pride marches are symbolic of this ideal for the LGBT [sic] community. These symbols mark us as a community that aspires to dissolve boundaries based on traditional identity markers'.[8] Of course, this willingness to dissolve boundaries upon which the architecture of oppression and privilege is placed is precisely what those opposed to queer communities are most afraid of – and why such an effort is made to split LGBTQI up into its constituent parts.[9] Making reference to Galatians, Cheng notes that 'to the extent that the church is one body that is made up of people of many sexualities, genders, and races, we can understand the church as a place that dissolves the traditional boundaries that divide us from one another'.[10]

There are few places in modern society where people from such radically different backgrounds might sit together on a pew, sing together, read together, eat and drink together, beyond the church. 'This gathering up of God's people ... is the work of the Holy Spirit and is a way of returning us to the radical love that was sent by the first person of the Trinity, and the radical love that was recovered by the second person of the Trinity', says Patrick Cheng.[11] There is, then, an implicit

8 Patrick Cheng, *Radical Love* p.106
9 A particularly silly example of this was at the General Synod of the Church of England in February 2023, when a lay member attempted to dissect the acronym LGBTQI+ in a series of amendments, apparently failing to see the irony in such a move taking place in the context of a motion calling for the church to 'lament and repent of the failure of the Church to be welcoming to LGBTQI+ people'. The Report of Proceedings – a depressing read – is available here: https://www.churchofengland.org/sites/default/files/2023-07/updated-report-of-proceedings-feb-2023.pdf [accessed October 7th 2023].
10 Patrick Cheng, *Radical Love* p.106
11 Ibid

queerness to the church, however much it might want to avoid the use of that term.

Liz Edman develops this even further in her discussion of 'queer virtue'. She suggests that:

> … because queer virtue is so visible in our world – much as those gathered on that first Palm Sunday would have been shockingly visible to everyone around them – it provides a model that one can observe, ponder, and emulate. This is a model that could help Christians better understand how and why we live the way we do; but also, very importantly, it is a model that can help more of us proclaim our faith in words and deeds more powerfully, with greater consequence.[12]

She suggests that both Christians and queer people learn to 'participate in communities that demand integrity within ourselves, require justice in our dealings with one another, and look to the margins to address individual/communal/global degradation and suffering'.[13] It is without doubt that the church, if it wishes to better embody this vision, has much to learn from queer people and queer communities. If it is willing to do so, it may find that the transformation is bidirectional, enacted by unexpected grace.

QUEER CATHOLICITY

In our second chapter, when discussing the different meanings of queerness and their impact upon theology, we referred to 'Catholic Queering – a commitment to the catholic faith, yet a commitment that does not fear for the collapse of that faith if questions are asked of it'. It has been this method that has been pursued during this book – seeking not to demolish

---

[12] Elizabeth Edman, *Queer Virtue* p.165
[13] Ibid

all that there is, but to interrogate it and in the process aim to refine it, pointing to ways that the church might better live out its central vision. Here, it is worth revisiting why we undertook such a process.

Arguments between the different wings of the church(es) are endless, and amongst these are found debates on whether churches are more catholic, more protestant, more reformed, or anything in between. There is neither the time (nor does the author have the patience!) to debate these in length here, but a good yardstick for an historical understanding of the church would be to focus on its Four Marks – that it is 'one, holy, catholic, and apostolic'. The purpose of queering the church – certainly using the method here – is to work for a church that *more fully* embodies these marks. Queering is a process which intends to strip away those things that make the church less holy, less catholic, less apostolic – and ultimately, less 'one'. Each of these four marks interacts with one another – and a church that excludes the queer is unable to truly call itself any of the four marks. A church cannot be one or holy if it others queer people; it cannot be catholic or apostolic if it is dressed in robes of patriarchal cis-heteronormativity. We see here, then, the interwoven nature of the queering exercise.

Unfortunately, 'catholicity' has become all too often associated with the repetition of vain actions and 'doing things a particular way' rather than with a way of engaging with the faith – in other words, a particular positionality when regarding the sources of theology. Far too much emphasis has been placed on the externalities of the faith rather than what they embody, meaning that these externalities have taken on the label of 'catholic' whilst very little attention is given to what they actually signify. We therefore tend towards an outward set of actions whose form is entirely separated from the original nature and meaning of their inner reality, and this is especially the case when we consider the sacraments. A determination to hold on to a 'catholic' version of marriage in which 'catholic' ultimately means man and woman demeans the word catholic – it is merely an appeal to form and not to substance. Queerness, on the other hand, allows us to focus on substance – and do so in a way that allows us to move beyond the way this substance is expressed in practical terms. It allows us to find the truly catholic by enabling us to look beyond the human window dressing and to seek to see things on God's terms rather than our own.

A church that is committed to being one, holy, catholic and apostolic, is a church that is open to rediscovery, to renewal, and to reform, yet not on arbitrary grounds but by paying proper attention to the real that speaks of God. It is simply not enough to equate catholicism with conservatism – conservatism is not a neutral mode, but one that is based on a choice of what to conserve. Our decision on what to conserve, what to refine, what to interrogate, and what to jettison, is a decision that queerness helps us make, by forcing us to focus on the real, that embodies and enables the one, holy, catholic and apostolic. Queerness may be appear to be a doctrine of rupture, yet it is rupture in the external and peripheral in order to make way again for the continuity of the eternal in a continual process of refinement, interrogation and attention.[14]

AN ANGLICAN CRISIS

It is not only in the Church of England or the wider Anglican Communion that matters of sex, sexuality, gender, and intimacy are matters of great disagreement, but it does appear that churches under the Anglican umbrella are tending towards a period of significant crisis. Triggering such a crisis,[15] however,

---

[14] Queerness might aid us in a variety of ways, enabling us to make use of processes such as *ressourcement* and *aggiornamento* but also teasing out where there may indeed be a valid and reasonable development of doctrine. In both cases, the key gift of queerness is to start with the real and not the imagined, and to ask what God is doing in, through, and for the real situations in human lives and the real ontology of human persons.

[15] Or, rather, recognising that we are in the midst of it!

is not a bad thing, if such a crisis can end up being fruitful and – indeed – procreative. The Anglican theological method is a gift to the wider church, and yet has become increasingly side-lined in both the Church of England and the wider Communion. The time to reclaim this ground is now – and queerness can be part of the toolbox to do so.

The refinement and interrogation of doctrine should be central to any Anglican theological enterprise, and we should have the confidence to recognise that nothing is harmed by the mere asking of questions. It would be a capricious God – and a callous one, at that – who becomes upset and offended at the human endeavour of questioning the world and all that is in it, and even questioning God Godself. Indeed, such a God would not only be capricious and callous, but utterly un-Biblical and illogical, too, since God created human beings with the capacity for rational thought, giving us the very ability to question that allows us to engage ever more deeply with the reality of human life and our place in the palm of God's hand.

Queerness, then, not only acts as a corrective to the worship of the normative, but in so doing liberates theology itself to allow it to fulfil its potential. It offers a fruitful vision that challenges the smallness of the ideological vision put forward by cis-heteronormativity, and encourages us to explore this vision, whatever is thrown at those of us with the courage to do so. It calls us to remember that people are ends in themselves and not means to an end, and all such people, queer or otherwise, are part of a real creation which God calls 'very good'. So perhaps the time for a good crisis is upon us, if only to allow the fruits of the Spirit found in queerness as a method, and queer people themselves, to dance again on the face of the Earth, and through them to see the handiwork of the Creator. Perhaps it is time – at last – for us to embrace our queer gifts.

11

QUEER GIFTS

In recent years, the Genesis creation stories have spent far too much time being wielded as weapons in order to bash queer people. We have touched on this a few times in the course of this book, and it is clear that the last arguments against queer people having a lived out and integrated social-sexual life now hinge on the alleged creation of humankind as *either* male or female, with each of these having their own discrete, categorical place in the created order, unchanging and immovable. Our thesis throughout has been to reject that as fundamentally *unreal* – as fundamentally make-believe. We have done this from the scientific viewpoint, and we have done it from the theological viewpoint. Now, in our final few pages, let us turn to Genesis itself and allow it to be lifegiving not only to those who fit within the cis-heteronormative prison, but to all of God's children. How might we meet Genesis and rejoice as the queer beloved?

'Let us make humans in our own image', says God – and it was so: 'God created humans[1] in his own image, in the image of God he created them'. God created both male *and* female in his image – Genesis 1 not giving a temporality to the creation of man and woman, but simply stating that humans – *adam* – were made in God's image, humans irrespective of their sex, with male and female, and everything

---

[1] Interestingly the Hebrew is 'adam', thus 'adam' was made in the image of God, 'male *and* female'.

in between, being made in the 'image of God'. Having made humankind, 'God blessed them'. In Genesis 2, God creates a helper (in a similar meaning to 'God is my helper' that we find later in scripture) as 'bone of [Adam's] bones, and flesh of [Adam's] flesh'. These two – from the same substance, the same very bone and flesh itself, cleave to one another 'and they become one flesh'.

Here, in the primordial times, they 'were both naked and were not ashamed'. Here, the use of sex as power has not yet reared its head. Here is innocence, where humankind, made of the same substance and in the image and likeness of God, simply *is*, delighting in its createdness and in the garden of its Creator. Flesh – itself from the same source – cleaves and clings to itself, as humankind finds unity in companionship and relationship with humankind, as it is not good for them to be alone (on Earth). Humankind chooses humankind – and in doing so, chooses the very image of God their creator. 'God saw everything that he had made, and indeed, it was very good'.

These are the stories we tell ourselves about ourselves – who we have been, who we are, who we will be. These are stories of mythology and of meaning, of beauty and of longing. These are stories where humanity is first closest to God, before humanity moves away and forms its own ideologies, its own idols, and demands the power and authority that can only lead to loss and sadness, and away from our relationship with the source of life. Here is our beginning, yet a time that we humans walk away from, to build our own empires and turn our desire away from the image of God to the creations of humankind.[2] Our closeness to God will only come back

---

[2] If readers might forgive a brief foray into queer apologetics: The Fall is far too often used as a way to distinguish the entirely 'good' from the entirely 'bad' (here again we meet the need for categorisation) – and hence can be used in a rather circular way to condemn we don't like about the world as being somehow the result of The Fall. The Fall may make humankind imperfect – but it cannot legitimately be used to describe some human beings' *essence* as 'bad' simply because we don't like it. As we have seen, queerness is not like a hat you take off and put back on again – it is deeply wired into our very being as humans, and is not a wilful rebellion against

through redemption – a redemption wrought by the very Image of God in Jesus Christ, fully human and fully divine – a redemption brought about through an act of utter self-giving love, the love that sits at the heart of our very being, and is the very essence of God. In redemption, our disintegrated selves are brought back together – our holiness is restored – our Image, marred by sin and grief and human wilfulness, is once again made aright. We walk redeemed, not because of what we have done, but because of what God has done. We walk redeemed, in the light of the resurrection, as embodied humankind – beloved, and each one of us precious to the God of the universe.

Such is our faith – such is the faith of the church. Such is the faith of the straight, the bi, the lesbian, or the gay, the intersex, the asexual, the trans or the cis, the Two Spirit, the gender non-conforming, the gender-fluid, the non-binary, the questioning and the queer. Such is the faith of us all – all of us created in flesh, all of us redeemed, all of us called to resurrection hope, through faith, in love. God sees that it is very good. God does not demand that we pluck something integral to ourselves out of ourselves, and if we wish to know how we might flourish, God gives us the tools we have outlined in this book to determine precisely that. As uncomfortable as it might be for some, God works out God's purposes through queer lives just the same as any others – and God's working out of those purposes does not require us to become less than ourselves in order to do so.

God. To allege that this essence is therefore a result of the Fall (the usual language being about 'disordered' desires as a standalone issue) is to make an argument that is backed up by neither scripture, tradition, or reason. If we look at queerness without the cis-heteronormative paradigm being front and centre, then we ask questions about flourishing, goodness, holiness, and our ability to label it as 'wholly bad' becomes significantly weaker. The narratives within the conservative spheres of the church who claim that queerness is the result of the Fall should really be seen more as a politicisation of the Fall in the project to 'conserve' the patriarchal values within the society, rather than as a theological in and of itself.

Queerness, then, is about bringing our whole selves to God and presenting them as a living sacrifice, holy and acceptable to God, which is our reasonable worship (Romans 12). Just like everyone else, we are called not to be conformed to this age or its ideologies, but to be transformed by the renewing of the mind, so that we may discern what is the will of God – what is good and acceptable and perfect. We are called to let love be genuine, to love one another with mutual affection, outdoing one another in showing honour). We are called to be ardent in spirit, serve the Lord, be patient in affliction, and persevere in prayer. We are called to contribute to the needs of the saints and pursue hospitality to strangers. We are called, too, to bless those who persecute us, and not to become overcome by evil, but instead to overcome evil with good.

Our queerness is that blessing, a blessing that is offered to the church as a gift of the Holy Spirit who works in the world and animates God's church. Our queerness is part of the pro-creative stream into which we are called to participate. Our queerness reconnects the body and soul and mind, refusing to accept the cheap categorisations we humans wish existed. Our queerness shows that people cannot and must not be used as means to political ends, but are ends in and of themselves – entire, complete, made holy through the redeeming sacrifice of Jesus Christ.

REFINING THE QUEER

This book has unashamedly made the case for queerness. When we see good and godly things in the world, the church has been far too willing to look the other way, or call an apple an orange, and tied itself up in circular arguments, untruths, mistruths, and plain denials to give it the tools to do so. When the beauty of queer relationality or relationships have been clear as day, the church has called it disordered and unholy. We have tried, time and again, to mar the Image of God in queer people – but we, the church, have failed. The time for change is upon us.

However, this does not take away the serious questions about how to interpret and understand Biblical sexual ethics. Queerness is not a free-for-all, or an excuse to do nothing. It is a calling to mind, a calling to attention of reality – and a way of asking what really matters, and what really exists in order for it to matter. It is a way – however varied, by its nature – of helping us move beyond human ideologies to try, however faltering, to lose our human lenses and instead follow the voice of the Spirit. Far too much of our ethics to date has been based on human readings of the Bible that do no justice to the Spirit of God who breathed through its authors and vivifies the church today. Too much of our ethics is based on respectability, and prudishness, and normativity. Too much of our ethics is based on implications which themselves are built on unsure ground.

Yet all this being said, queer culture itself is no panacea (nor is it monolithic), and also – in what seems to be a paradoxical way – needs to be queered.[3] Our lives, loves, and communities as queer people have much to say to the church, but this is a dialogue – a dialogue that must itself be queered. The antagonism between church and queer has been fomented and fed by the church, and it is no small wonder that so many queer people wouldn't wish to cross the threshold of a church. Yet we know that queer Christians exist, and we know that there is nothing anti-queer about the faith, even if there is about some of its proponents (and conversely, there is nothing anti-faith in the queer or in queering). Queer culture needs Christ just as any other

---

[3] There are, for example, genuine questions to be asked about the overt sexualisation found within some parts of queer culture, with a focus on youth and ideas of physical beauty, some White queer cultures' rejection of the non-White, some gay male cultures rejection of the female, non-binary, or trans*, and so on. The aim is not to replace one cultural hegemony with another, but to interrogate and refine what has developed and ask what of God might be found in it.

culture does, yet as a culture that has been shut out and hated by the church (and, indeed, in some ways has itself been shaped by that rejection, in ways good and bad), the church needs to be the one who makes the approach, in humility and repentance. Queer culture needs to be open to being refined by the Holy Spirit, but the church needs to do the leg work to make dialogue possible. A single Synodical apology is not going to do that.

BEYOND MONOGAMY?

This leads us to a discussion of some of the things which we have, perhaps, skirted around during our conversations on sexual intercourse and expression. We have thought in some detail about the covenantal nature of casual sex, but we must also be willing to ask whether – even if it might be theologically defensible – on balance it should be so defended. One of the first questions we need to answer is whether there does indeed need to be a Christian sexual ethic – and if so, what the purpose and bounds of this ethic are. Indeed, taking a step back and recognising that our sex lives can be places where similar actions can have different meanings, can there really be such a thing as a single sexual ethic? To what extent should a church be proclaiming and how much should it be listening and grappling? Should the church be solemnising marriage, or any kind of relationship at all? What is the purpose of such an ecclesial event? To what degree should all our sexual experiences be reflective of God in the same way?[4]

These questions matter, because despite the rather bubble-like life experience that many bishops appear to (or rather, claim to) live in, the kind of sex the church talks about is just the tip of the iceberg. We have spoken about

---

[4] We touched on this in Chapter 7 in our discussion of masturbation, for example.

kink previously, but we might also think of open relationships, polyamory,[5] orgies, sex parties, swinging, and so on – some of which are versions of covenant (albeit in ways that are different to monogamous covenants) and some of which express covenant in what might appear to be a radically different way to that as traditionally understood by the church. Of course, the knee-jerk reaction is to throw up arms in horror and bewail the destruction of the Christian society, but this is hardly a helpful response[6] – and nor does it pay attention to the theological questions and dynamics at play in such relationships. Whilst it may be uncomfortable to some in the church, it is by no means clear that the theological qualities that we find and rejoice in, in monogamous coupled relationships, cannot be reflected in other forms of relationship. That is not the same as suggesting absolute equivalence in these different forms of relationship (although we must, surely, be open to that as a result of our deliberations), but it is a demand that we engage with these questions seriously, and theologically. Once again, something not being 'for us' does not mean that there is not something of God in it, and we must be careful not to merely replace cis-heteronormative ideology with monogamous ideology.[7] First and foremost, we must be dealing in theology and not ideology – and theology really does not always have all the answers to hand!

The only way that we will do justice to these kind of questions – and just as importantly, to the people involved – is if we approach this process as a discussion and a dialogue,

---

[5] Which is, incidentally, fundamentally different to the patriarchally-based practice of polygamy. This in itself does, perhaps, warrant a theological exploration, but is too often conflated by those who benefit from 'shock factor theology'. Karen Keen (*Scripture, Ethics and the Possibility of Same-Sex Relationships* p.32) offers an interesting discussion of Jesus' intentionality (or otherwise) in the use of 'two' in St Mark's Gospel which may or may not have relevance for our discussions here.

[6] Even in the chamber of the General Synod of the Church of England.

[7] That is not to say that we might not end up defending monogamy as the right context for covenantal relationships theologically – but there is something important here about doing so by engaging with it theologically rather than ideologically or in a knee-jerk manner.

in which the church learns to listen and discern together. At the same time as listening, we need to ask questions of human experience – why, for example, do humans appear to tend towards intimate, exclusive, romantic relationships? What does this have to do with God? To what extent should the will be tamed, and why? How freely does consent sit in questions of human non-exclusive sexual relationships? Who, if anyone, is being hurt – and how do we know? Are people in open or polyamorous relationships because they want to be, because it best helps them flourish, or for other reasons? How might we think sensibly about the clash of covenants in open relationships – are the people involved inadvertently partitioning some part of our social-sexual selves out and doing harm to themselves because of it? Or is it possible to engage in different forms of sexual expression concurrently – might the sharing of the sexual encounter with a third person (or more) actually build up the relationship of the couple?

We must be willing to ask and seek to answer these kinds of questions, however contingently – most particularly the 'why' – and then place them into dialogue with our theology. It is true that once we approach sex, sexuality and gender from a queer perspective, then we open up a huge number of questions, but that is because we are approaching the real rather than the make-believe. It is not that these questions do not exist when we approach with the prison of cis-heteronormativity – rather, we are simply sticking our fingers in our ears and shouting so we cannot hear them.

Throughout, then, we need to have our theological minds engaged and never stop asking the 'why' of proponents and opponents of these different forms of sexual expression. For example, in her book *Holiness and Desire*,[8] Jessica Martin outlines some of the graces we associate with marriage – a 'love-project' which she suggests is given the space in 'the exclusive two-person unit of marriage that 'emulates

---

[8] Jessica Martin, *Holiness and Desire* (London: Canterbury Press, 2020) p.128

the steady and complete attention of God. She describes it as developing 'mutual knowledge' that is 'essentially, and perhaps mercifully out of reach'; it is 'wrested by grace, indeed by miracle, from an impossible set of demands in an impossible context'; it is 'a discipline of love in and of itself … one of the means by which we learn the nature of the sacrificial, the generous, by which we pursue the lifelong vocation to learn another person as well as we possibly can, good and bad, through all the extraordinary changes wrought by time and change and ageing and sickness, along with the betrayals of sin, all the way to the final change of death, to and beyond and through the constant experience of loss'. Such a description is overflowing with the theological depth and richness that 'marriage is between a man and a woman' so sorely lacks, and yet itself requires questions asked of it as to why these very graces cannot be experienced in, for example, polyamorous relationships. She continues:

> Marriage is one of the ways we might have a glimpse of the cost involved in the project of time-bound loving, but also of the vastness of its blessing. In it we could learn both to know and to bear to be known, so that at the last we might be assisted to endure and embrace the weight of God's particular and personal knowledge with hope, and faith, and love.

Our ultimate question, perhaps, is whether we might be willing to find ourselves open to other ways beyond monogamous relationships, as well – and if not, why?

THE CHURCH AS DISCIPLINARIAN

Here, then, might be a good time to return to the inadequacy of the church's engagement with issues of sex, sexuality, and gender more generally. Not only are the questions we are willing to ask too limited, and the theological work so shallow, but our entire approach is so focused on rules that we end up acting as though there is no complexity in human life. In the Church of England, since the introduction of *Issues in Human Sexuality* in 1991 (and its somewhat mysterious development into a disciplinary document ruling over the lives of clergy), there has been a deeply ahistorical and theologically indefensible position advanced, that set 'rules' for the clergy that bore little to no relation to the expectations placed (or rather, the expectations proffered for the reception or otherwise) on lay people. We will not detain ourselves for long here except to note how representative this rules-based approach has become in the way churches have engaged with such questions, meaning that the church's prime position appears to be one of disciplinarian, with such discipline primary resting on some notion of sexual propriety rather than a lived out understanding of relationality.

Such a rules-based approach may be beneficial to those seeking to either enforce it, or ensure others are punished because of it, but it leads to some very bizarre outcomes. In the Church of England, sexual 'impropriety' has become a common cause of clergy discipline, with rules that have developed which appear to do little more than hurt everyone involved.[9] It is not clear, for example, why 'sexual misdemeanour' should be afforded such severity in church discipline when other failures that relate to fidelity, honesty, appropriate relationships, and so on, are not. Even clergy found to be using dating apps are frequently censured, with an apparent failure to recognise that such apps may not solely be for the purpose of soliciting sex.

---

[9] We might think here even of the case of adultery by clergy – whilst it is entirely understandable that the church might indeed take some proper interest in this kind of situation, the current disciplinary procedures are likely to punish the wronged spouse as much, if not more, than the person committing adultery. Clergy may indeed lose their role and thus their livelihood and home – yet very little is done to prevent the negative impact on the spouse, which seems extraordinarily unjust.

Yet two other situations make this issue clearer, both of which relate to clergy (over whom the church has some authority). The first is that there is an apparent requirement for clergy to enter into legally recognised unions even if the church itself officially opposes the existence of these very legal entities – for example marriage between those of the same-sex or gender, or civil partnership. For years, clergy could lose their licenses for entering into a marriage with someone of the same sex or gender, but under new regulations, clergy instead appear to lose their license if they *don't* do so – a bizarre turn of events, not least because the legal is being afforded a moral status without any clear reasoning whatsoever. The second is the continued opposition of the church to clergy co-habiting without being married – a prohibition that appears to be based more on cultural norms than on even the slightest reflection on not only relationship but also the possibility of cohabiting without having sexual intercourse! This prohibition is little more than the work of cis-heteronormativity – albeit a Victorian expression of it – and would be laughable if it didn't express so clearly how far the church needs to come in its discussions on these topics.

We will turn to the need for the transformation of the church as we move into our final chapter. For now, though, let us turn back to the positive impact that queerness can have, and indeed does have, on the church. Rather than looking askance at queer people, or at the very best trying to welcome them to the table of cis-heteronormativity, what might queer people gift to a church so desperately in need of freedom?

QUEER GIFTS

Queer people are quite remarkable, given all they have been subject to and continue to be subjected to, and queer Christians are no exception. The church has spent decades trying to stifle and silence them, and yet not only are they still here, but they are still giving back to a church that has too frequently presented them with a scorpion instead of an egg. Queer people still turn up, still serve the church – including as ordained ministers – and far too often this very fact is forgotten. For all the talk of queer people trying to 'destroy the church', the reality is that they are amongst its most loyal servants, despite everything thrown at them.

Indeed, that experience of being on the margins and on the edge is, perhaps, one of the reasons that queer people are so impactful in their ministry, ordained or lay. It remains extraordinary that God appears to be calling so many queer people to be deacons, priests, and bishops in God's church – particularly if they are really as 'disordered' as their opponents would suggest![10] Queer people's persistence against the odds and their continued dwelling on the margins – where Christ Himself dwelt without always demanding the margins retreated to the centre – means that the church's worship of the normative does not remain, at least in some cases, unchallenged. Queer presence at the Eucharist reminds the church that it does not own the sacrament, however much it wishes that it did, and the baptism of queer people brings us back to the Image of God, rather than the image of normativity.[11]

The honesty and courage of queer people in the face of often deafening abuse and vitriol is a sign of the Kingdom of Heaven, queer solidarity being a sign of hope that cannot be silenced come what may. In coming out, queer people show this courage,[12] and in simply being themselves, they

[10] It remains ludicrous, for example, that under Pope Benedict XVI those with 'deep-seated' homosexual tendencies were forbidden from becoming priests (an example can be found here: https://www.independent.co.uk/news/world/europe/pope-restates-ban-on-gay-priests-and-says-homosexuality-is-disordered-517522.html [accessed October 7th 2023]). One wonders quite how successful this was in practice.

[11] The church is, of course, minster and custodian of these things, but this comes with a responsibility, and any authority there is, is purely participatory in God's authority.

[12] Some queer theologians have even gone so far as to talk of coming out as itself sacramental.

challenge the unreality that the church continues to promote. Queer families and queer community shows the church so much it appears to have forgotten about the value of friendship, honesty, and solidarity, and in their awkwardness in the face of the endless desire for respectability, queer people call the church back to its very essence, revealing it once again as having the potential to be the disruptive vehicle of the Holy Spirit. Queer people, so often described in terms of sin, themselves embody these virtues, helping the church not only to remember who she is, but to be refined and restored as one, holy, catholic and apostolic.

Queer people and the queerness they embody have so much to offer if only the church would recognise what is happening in her midst. Queerness demands refinement and interrogation of our doctrines and our dogmas, of our firmly held beliefs and our deep-seated practices. It calls the church to embrace all the sources of theology, and to do so in a way that is excited by discovery and not suspicious of it. Queerness smashes the arbitrary, human-designed and enforced categories that suck life out rather than breathe life into human existence. Queerness challenges the church to move beyond the secular norm and re-embrace the sacred and the holy in the world and in the people that God has created for Godself.

'When lived out with integrity, the ethical impulse of our communities is not a demand for respectability, but rather is a call to authenticity,' says Liz Edman in her discussion of LGBTQI communities.[13] This ethical impulse is the very impulse our church needs to embody and learn to desire. Queer people are in the church because Christianity itself is fundamentally queer – and it is through queer people that the cis-heteronormative ideology will finally be crushed and destroyed, if only we would let it be so. As Marcella Althaus-Reid puts it, 'the theological scandal is that bodies speak, and God speaks through them ... queerness is something

---

[13] Elizabeth Edman, *Queer Virtue* p.96

that belongs to God, and ... people are divinely Queer by grace'.[14]

Linn Tonstad builds on this very point. 'Queerness is *God's*; we become queer *by grace*. Bodies speak, and that speech is also God's. God is not a tidy God, categorising God's people neatly and expecting them to stay within such categories'.[15] Here, then, is the challenge of embracing queerness, and yet also its greatest gift – the offer made to God's creatures to allow themselves to find themselves as graced into queerness, as embodied manifestations of that grace which does not demand we categorise ourselves except to say that we are children of the beautiful, loving God who created each and every one of us, each in our glorious, absurd, astounding diversity, in God's own image, who looks on us and calls us very good, and who calls us to dance in this grace in the eternity of the overflowing, abundant love of God. For such is queer redemption.

[14]   Marcella Althaus-Reid *The Queer God* (London: Routledge, 2003) pp.33-34 quoted in Linn Tonstad *Queer Theology* p.92
[15]   Linn Tonstad, *Queer Theology* p.92

12

THE LAZARUS CHURCH

How our church needs to hear that clarion call of grace.
Yet how we, too, are called to embody something beyond ourselves.

We – in the Church of England, in the wider Anglican Communion, and in the church more widely – have a big problem. In fact, we have a number of big problems, some bigger than others. Throughout this book, we have thought about one of them in particular: the way that queer people have been endlessly victimised and abused by a church that they continue to love and serve despite everything. Yet queer theology, as we said right at the start, is neither simply about allowing people to get married, nor is it simply about LGBTQI people – even though it holds the key to their liberation. It is a much wider project than that, and a work of the Holy Spirit.

Queerness, if it is to reach its potential, cannot stop at the liberation of gay men. This much seems obvious, and yet far too often what is described as 'queer friendly' is in fact simply gay men friendly. Nor can it stop at the liberation of young people – the LGBTQI community continues to face challenges in this regard, like wider society, and merely replacing one ideology – cis-heteronormativity – with another normativity of age is to fundamentally fail in the queering agenda. Similarly, queering cannot stop at the liberation of White people, or able-bodied people, or cis people. None of this is true queering, and none of it does justice to the work of the Spirit that queering seeks to be. Queering demands an end to arbitrary categorisation, and this does not stop at sex, sexuality and gender.

As we have seen, our church narratives have subverted reality time after time, and far too often we hear that all liberals and queers are White, and all black people are conservatives (an interesting non-mirroring), with liberal White queers as the enemies of conservative Black heterosexuals. As Patrick Cheng says, 'this is particularly true when society wants these two groups to be pitted against each other, as has been the case with the marriage equality movement. This, of course, renders queer people of colour as nonexistent'.[1] In too many of our church and societal conversations, Black queers are ignored, not least by White queers, and their struggles and triumphs are Whitewashed out of the record. Disabled people, queer or otherwise, are entirely absent from much of church dialogue. Women remain the unseen majority.

It doesn't need to be this way, and as those who have faced our own oppression and victimisation at the hands of a normative ideology, we are duty bound not only to fight for our liberation but for the liberation of all those who suffer under this yoke. Cis-heteronormativity is but one face of a wider normative ideology that we are all – whether it directly affects us, and how it directly affects us – called to fight against as Christians. It is, quite simply, an imperative for us because that normativity seeks to displace Christ as Head of the Church. It seeks, through its conscious and unconscious disciples, to lull us into a church of the comfortable, to encourage us to submit to it, to place our trust in it, to eat its bread and to leave the wilderness in return for all the kingdoms of the world. It demands that we replace the real with the unreal.

Such a worshipped idol of normativity is, perhaps, the inevitable result of the Constantinian shift, and Constantinian

---

[1] Patrick Cheng, *Radical Love* p.73

cultural Christianity. If we remain siloed in our own individual theologies of liberation without seeing their need for collaboration and integration – their need for intersectionality – then we will simply move the dial of normativity rather than smash it to pieces. Queer theology calls us to refuse this thin gruel, and instead to lay our own selves open to transformation in the refining fire of the Holy Spirit. We must be willing to let this Spirit penetrate and purify our lives – our whole selves – and we must be willing to commit ourselves to a life that is more journey than destination, a continuous learning about ourselves and others, with an endless openness to being corrected and cajoled. This is the way of queer holiness, of sanctification in the Holy Spirit. This is the way of queer redemption – for within us all remain the seeds of hope yet also the seeds of others' despair, and it is for the Son of Man to cleanse us and set us free if only we would let Him in.

THE LAZARUS CHURCH

He cried with a loud voice, 'Lazarus, come out!' The dead man came out, his hands and feet bound with strips of cloth and his face wrapped in a cloth. Jesus said to them, 'Unbind him, and let him go.'

John 11: 43-44

This is not, unsurprisingly, the first book in which the raising of Lazarus appears to strike a chord for LGBTQI Christians.[2] Indeed, it requires very little subtlety to see the way that Jesus' call to the dead man to 'come out' of the tomb might find echoes in the life of queer people more generally. Yet perhaps this passage speaks as much to the moribund and

---

[2] The recent book by the remarkable Roman Catholic Jesuit priest James Martin SJ, *Come Forth: The Raising of Lazarus and the Promise of Jesus' Greatest Miracle* (New York: HarperCollins, 2023), is a good starting point if readers want to explore this further.

exhausted church as it does to queer people – a church entombed in indifference, in failure, in fear, in disappointment, and yet a church entombed, too, in power, in normativity, in modes of oppression and structural violence. As that church comes out of the tomb, surely we are all called to unbind her, and let her go.

Through queerness we can begin that process of enrichening and enlivening a church brought low through its own disordered orientation, an orientation that looks towards the things of man rather than the things of God. By removing that cloth from the church's face, we might begin the process of repentance and recognition so desperately needed for her rebirth. As the bandages are removed, we might again embrace a church that delights in its weirdness, in its queerness, set free from its capture by the sweet murmurings of secular propriety. We might help the Lazarus church to vest its quest for truth in contingency, blinking in the light of day, dancing and singing in the beauty of holiness that surrounds it. Here we might hear its theology as music and poetry, as reflections of the holiness of the God who loves the world into being, as an agora of delight in which we search together for the right questions to give us a glimpse of the reality of life.

> *For as the earth brings forth its shoots*
> *and as a garden causes what is sown in it to spring up,*
> *so the Lord God will cause righteousness and praise*
> *to spring up before all the nations.*
>
> Isaiah 61:11

The church will one day embrace queerness, because ultimately the church, and all creation, is already queer. For now, the death-throes of the old order of normativity are heard, as humankind feels its power seeping away. Yet queerness will surely, day by day, softly perhaps yet unmistakably, build into an irresistible torrent of truth, a torrent in which each and every Christian is called to participate. As queerness, created and procreated, streams forward, so the church will be handed back – falteringly, yet beautifully; back to the God who sustains her and all her children, in whose service is perfect freedom.

> *O Israel, trust in the LORD; for with the LORD there is mercy, and with him is plenteous redemption.*
>
> Psalm 130:7

FOR FURTHER READING

Althaus-Reid, M., *Indecent Theology: Theological perversions in sex, gender and politics* (Oxford: Routledge, 2000)

Althaus-Reid, M., ed., *Liberation Theology and Sexuality* (Aldershot: Ashgate, 2006)

Althaus-Reid, M., *The Queer God* (London: Routledge, 2003)

Althaus-Reid, M., 'Thinking Theology and Queer Theory', *Feminist Theology* 15 (2007) pp.302-14

Bell, C. J. M., *Queer Holiness* (London: Darton, Longman and Todd, 2022)

Case, S-E., ed., *Performing Feminisms: Feminist Critical Theory and Theatre* (Baltimore, MD: Johns Hopkins, 1990)

Cheng, P., *Radical Love: An Introduction to Queer Theology* (New York: Seabury, 2011)

Collins, A. Y., 'Ethics in Paul and Paul in Ethics', *Journal of Biblical Literature* Vol 142:1 (2023) pp.6-21

Davison, A., *Blessing* (London: Canterbury Press, 2014)

Davison, A. *Why Sacraments?* (Westmont, IL: InterVarsity, 2013)

Edman, E. M., *Queer Virtue: What LGBTQ People Know About Life and Love and How It Can Revitalize Christianity* (Boston, MA: Beacon, 2016)

Ford, M., *God, Gender, Sex and Marriage* (London: Jessica Kingsley, 2019)

Greenough, C., *Queer Theologies: The Basics* (Oxford: Routledge, 2020)

Harries, R., 'The Anglican acceptance of contraception', *Transformation* Vol. 13:3 pp.2-4

Helminiak, D., *Sex and the Sacred: Gay Identity and Spiritual Growth* (Binghampton, NY: Harrington Park, 2006)

Loughlin, G., ed., *Queer Theology: Rethinking the Western Body* (Oxford: Blackwell, 2007)

Keen, K., *Scripture, Ethics and The Possibility of Same-Sex Relationships* (Grand Rapids, MI: Eerdmans, 2018)

Martin SJ, J., *Come Forth: The Raising of Lazarus and the Promise of Jesus's Greatest Miracle* (New York: HarperCollins, 2023)

Martin, J., *Holiness and Desire* (London: Canterbury Press, 2020)

Reynolds, P., *How Marriage Became One of the Sacraments: The Sacramental Theology of Marriage from its Medieval Origins to the Council of Trent* (Cambridge: CUP, 2016)

Song, R., *Covenant and Calling: Towards a Theology of Same-Sex Relationships* (London: SCM Press, 2014)

Tonstad, L. M., *Queer Theology: Beyond Apologetics* (Eugene, OR: Cascade, 2018)

Trible, P., *Texts of Terror: Literary-feminist Readings of Biblical Narratives* (Minneapolis, MN: Fortress, 1984)

Wilson, A., *More Perfect Union?: Understanding Same-sex Marriage* (London: Darton, Longman and Todd, 2014)

ACKNOWLEDGEMENTS

This book quite simply would not have happened had Queer Holiness not struck a chord. There are questions asked here which, frankly, many of us would prefer we didn't ask, yet I am grateful to those who have cajoled me and encouraged me in equal measure to get on and ask them. So many people have contributed to my thinking – but please believe me, the errors are all my own.

As ever, I am enormously grateful to the clergy and laity of St John the Divine, Kennington – most particularly to Fr Mark, who as my boss has tolerated my need to endlessly question the antics of the Church of England's House of Bishops. There really are few places like St John the Divine – it is a testament to the fact that catholic thought and practice do not require the surgical removal of one's brain. Vanessa and Jez are the most brilliant churchwardens, and without them, Deacon Annie, Fr Nick (and Ruth, and the boys!), Fr Peter, Fr Robert SSM, Bett, Ben, Ed, Kumba, Victor, Timi, and the whole host of others who keep the show on the road, St John the Divine would not be the beacon of hope that it is. To all of you, thank you.

I remain endlessly grateful to the Bishop of Southwark, Bishop Christopher Chessun, for his unwavering support and fatherly care. We are so blessed in our diocese to have someone whose ministry is so clearly one of service and love, and I am eternally grateful for his support in allowing me to be the awkward priest that I am.

There is no way I could have explored these issues in

as much detail if I had not been granted the opportunity to discuss all things queer across the pond. There are so many people to thank for making that happen – in particular Fr Matthew Gummess, Dr Julia Marvin, The Revd Stacy Alan, Bishop Deon Johnson, Canon Doris Westfall, Jillian Smith, Alexander Ames, Kristin Tadlock-Bell, Mary Alice Mouk, Dean Troy Mendez, Dean Matthew Woodward, The Revd Cameron Partridge, Fr Ian Davies, and the wonderful Dean Penny Bridges. I am enormously grateful, too, to Dean Pat Malloy and the Cathedral of St John the Divine in New York City, whose hospitality has been second to none. Pat has been an enormous encouragement – and is also enormous fun – and I am extremely grateful to him.

There are a few people closer to home who deserve special mention. I want to particularly thank Fr Tomos Reed for both his friendship and for his enquiring mind. This book would be nowhere near where it is without his helpful and sharp analysis – the church is extremely lucky to have people like him in its ranks. I am grateful, too, to Dr Emma Syea, Fr Calum Zuckert, Mthr Mae Christie, and the St Augustine's gang, and to Bishop David Hamid, Fr Neil Patterson, Prof Helen King, Jayne Ozanne, and all those working for change in the Church of England. We need it.

I'm grateful, too, to my Girton College colleagues, and to those at Oxleas NHS Foundation Trust with whom I've had the pleasure of working in the past few months. I have given up trying to neatly separate myself into priest or psychiatrist, and I hope this is not to the detriment of either vocation!

David Moloney and the team have once again been a brilliant support, and I am grateful to DLT for taking a punt on 'this kind of thing' and giving me an opportunity to ask the difficult questions which others would be all too happy to ignore.

As ever, my family have been wonderful. I'm sure I'm a bit of an enigma to them all, but they manage to conceal that with good grace and endure my idiosyncrasies without complaint. I am enormously grateful to them all, and most

ACKNOWLEDGEMENTS

particularly my mother, Kathryn. As I have said previously, I have also been welcomed into Piotr's family as a son, grandson, nephew, brother and friend, and their support and care has been wonderful and complete. Thank you to you all.

And Piotr – not only do you complete me in life, but you prove to be an excellent interlocutor in matters queer and have sharpened the arguments presented in this book to a major degree – my editor in all but name! I know working to my deadlines is something you sometimes endure rather than enjoy, but I cannot stress enough how much your contributions have made me think more carefully and attentively. All that said, the main reason I thank you is for being you – you are the world to me, and I hope you will always know that. Kocham Cię, babbington.

Charlie Bell
Feast of St John Henry Newman
October 2023